Introducing Microsoft Orleans

Implementing Cloud-Native Services
with a Virtual Actor Framework

Thomas Nelson

Apress®

Introducing Microsoft Orleans: Implementing Cloud-Native Services with a Virtual Actor Framework

Thomas Nelson
Louisville, KY, USA

ISBN-13 (pbk): 978-1-4842-8013-3
https://doi.org/10.1007/978-1-4842-8014-0

ISBN-13 (electronic): 978-1-4842-8014-0

Managing Director, Apress Media LLC: Welmoed Spahr
Acquisitions Editor: Joan Murray
Development Editor: Laura Berendson
Coordinating Editor: Jill Balzano

Cover image designed by Freepik (www.freepik.com)

Distributed to the book trade worldwide by Springer Science+Business Media LLC, 1 New York Plaza, Suite 4600, New York, NY 10004. Phone 1-800-SPRINGER, fax (201) 348-4505, e-mail orders-ny@springer-sbm. com, or visit www.springeronline.com. Apress Media, LLC is a California LLC and the sole member (owner) is Springer Science + Business Media Finance Inc (SSBM Finance Inc). SSBM Finance Inc is a **Delaware** corporation.

For information on translations, please e-mail booktranslations@springernature.com; for reprint, paperback, or audio rights, please e-mail bookpermissions@springernature.com.

Apress titles may be purchased in bulk for academic, corporate, or promotional use. eBook versions and licenses are also available for most titles. For more information, reference our Print and eBook Bulk Sales web page at http://www.apress.com/bulk-sales.

Any source code or other supplementary material referenced by the author in this book is available to readers on GitHub.

Printed on acid-free paper

As with every journey, it is never made alone.
I would like to thank those who have encouraged me to reach several
goals, including authoring this book that I now share with you.

Mom (Roxanne Lucas), you have cheered for me since day one.
You have always pushed me to better myself with love and support.
Thank you for everything. Without you,
I would not have been the person I am today.

Aaron Lucas, MD, your advice has never led me astray.
"This too shall pass," and it has. You took me in as your own and
taught me much. I am grateful for your counsel.

Dad (Vincent Nelson Jr.), without you, I would not be where I am
today. No matter the seriousness of a problem, you always find the
silver lining through humor and kindness.

Leo and Cora, my wonderful fur-kids, I treasure every day
we have together.

Cynthia F. C. Hill, PhD, you have single-handedly reconstructed my
writing. This book would not have come to fruition without your
guidance. You helped better my life.

Corey, Britney, Knox, Roscoe Cooley, you are my second family.
You have been my rock during difficult times and accepted me as
family. I always look forward to working on the next game dev jam.

Joan Murray and Jill Balzano, thank you for working with me
on this book. It has been a pleasure. This book would never have
happened without you both.

Micheal Kelly and Reece Schwegman, great friends, great advice, and
great times. You guys are irreplaceable.

Phuong Pham, Kevin Turner, Alex Olson, we are lifetime friends.
We have urged each other to do our best, sharing strength and calm.

My work friends: Dat Trinh, Karuna Byrd, Lorenzo Castro, Barry Chase, Keith Meyers, Hussein Rashid, and many others. Thank you for giving me the opportunity to fulfill my dream as a software architect. You each have taught me so much, which has helped me learn and expand to better myself. I am grateful for your time, support, and critical evaluations.

Mei Ying Tan, my counterpart in class, you have become a great friend and have brought out my academic competitive side. You make the classes exciting, and I am grateful we have met.

Lydia Pearce, Amy Rawson, Kiera, HBomb, Angel Ortiz, Dean Dusk, BunchiJumpi, Ha Nguyen, and Marissa Pelchat, thank you for your time, unwavering support, and wonderful friendship. The pandemic has been horrible; however, it did bring us together, and I am grateful to have each one of you in my life.

Table of Contents

About the Author xi

About the Technical Reviewer xiii

Acknowledgments.. xv

Introduction xvii

Chapter 1: A Primer on Microsoft Orleans and the Actor Model 1

Origins of Orleans 1

    Origins and Use Cases of Orleans 2

    Actor Model Explained.. 5

Actor Model Infused with Orleans.. 7

    Grain Lifecycle... 9

    Single Developer 10

Production Uses and History.. 12

Summary.. 14

Chapter 2: Introducing Microsoft Orleans 17

What Can Orleans Do for Us?... 17

Cloud-Native, Elastic, Highly Available 17

Common Use Cases for Actor Model Frameworks.. 18

Microsoft Orleans Base Libraries, Community, and Included Technologies 20

    Create and Maintain an Orleans Application as a Single Developer....................................... 20

    Community and Constant Advancements.. 22

    Multiple Hosting Solutions Are Supported... 23

    Resource Management and Expansion 23

    Failure Handling 24

    Streaming... 25

Persistence 26

Summary 26

Chapter 3: Lifecycles 29

Grain Lifecycle 29

    Grain Reentrancy 32

    External Tasks and Grains 33

    Grain Services 33

    Stateless Worker Grains 33

    Grain Call Filters 34

Silos 34

    Grain Directory 36

Message Path 37

    Development Setup 38

    Typical Configuration 38

    Silo Configuration 39

    Cluster 41

Silo Membership 41

Multi-clusters 42

    Gossip Protocol 43

    Journaled Grains 44

    Eventual Consistency 44

    Heterogeneous Silos 45

Summary 46

Chapter 4: Enhancing Current Designs 49

Overview 49

General Comparison 51

Elasticity and Availability Comparisons 55

Business Logic Complexity 59

Deployment 63

Summary 64

Chapter 5: Starting Development **67**

Overview 67

Composition 67

Building Our First Application.. 68

Grain Interface 72

Grain.. 72

Silo 73

Client.. 75

Grain Communication.. 82

Summary... 88

Chapter 6: Timers and Reminders **91**

Overview 91

Creating a Timer.. 92

Running the Timer... 95

Creating a Reminder 97

Setting Up an Azure Table 100

Running the Reminder 107

Summary.. 110

Chapter 7: Unit Tests.. **113**

Unit Test Summary... 113

Orleans Unit Testing Overview 114

Creating Our Unit Test Grain.. 116

Setting Up Our Test Cluster 117

Running the Test(s) 120

Adding the CallingGrain Test.. 121

Run the Unit Tests.. 122

Additional Testing 123

Summary.. 124

Chapter 8: The Orleans Dashboard **125**

Overview 125

Adding the Orlean Dashboard to Our Solution 125

Running the Dashboard 128

Additional Options 135

Expanding the Dashboard 136

Summary... 137

Chapter 9: Deployment **139**

Compatible Grains... 139

Database Handling (Deployment)... 141

Cluster Management... 141

CI/CD Overview 142

    Common Deployment Scenarios 145

Setting Up the Azure Environment 145

Walk-Through to Create a CI/CD Pipeline.. 146

    Initial Setup 146

Creating Resources with Azure CLI 147

Provisioning Scripts 148

    Pwsh_resource_provision.ps1 Code (PowerShell) 149

    Bash_resource_provision.sh Code (Command Line)...................... 150

    Provision Script Summary 151

Deployment Files 152

    Dockerfile 152

    Dockerfile Code 153

    Dockerfile Summary 153

    Deployment.yaml.. 154

    Deployment.yaml Code... 154

    Deployment.yaml File Summary... 157

Continuous Integration and Continuous Delivery Pipeline Creation 158

    Continuous-Integration.yaml 159

    Continuous-Integration.yaml Code 159

    Continuous-Integration.yaml Summary 161

    Continuous-delivery.yaml 161

    Continuous-delivery.yaml Code 162

    Continuous-delivery.yaml Summary 164

File Structure Validation 165

    Folders and Files Added 165

Secrets for Deployment 166

    Service Principle Name (SPN) 167

    Subscription ID 168

    Tenant ID 168

Adding Secrets to GitHub 169

Automated Deployment 170

    Trigger the Process 170

    View AKS Status on Azure Portal 171

    AKS Load Balancer 172

    Dashboard 173

    Deploy 173

    Additional Orleans Troubleshooting Information 173

Summary 174

Chapter 10: Conclusion 177

Origins 177

Introduction of Microsoft Orleans 178

Lifecycles 178

Comparisons 179

Project Structure 181

Timers and Reminders 182

TABLE OF CONTENTS

Unit Tests.. 183

Orleans Dashboard... 184

Deployment.. 186

Future Aspects 187

References.. **189**

Index.. **193**

About the Author

Thomas Nelson, Lead Cloud Architect and Microsoft Certified Azure Solutions Architect Expert, has worked in several technical fields spanning from the graphic design of websites to development and architecture. During his 10+ years of backend development, his interest has gravitated toward DevSecOps and automation. He is involved in core automation for cloud development and infrastructure for enterprises. He enjoys teaching others and is often found at local meetups presenting various technologies, patterns, and software examples. He is thrilled to be using Orleans and considers it one of those wonderful and valuable frameworks that should be in the tool kit of every architect and backend developer. Also, he is pleased to have extensive experience with monolithic and microservice systems to build cloud-native solutions, including actor framework back ends. He has an associate's degree in graphic design and bachelor's degree in computer information systems and is currently attending Harvard Extension School pursuing his master's degree in information management systems.

About the Technical Reviewer

 **Carsten Thomsen** is a backend developer primarily but working with smaller frontend bits as well. He has authored and reviewed a number of books and created numerous Microsoft Learn courses, all to do with software development. He works as a freelancer/contractor in various countries in Europe, with Azure, Visual Studio, Azure DevOps, and GitHub as some of his tools. Being an exceptional troubleshooter, asking the right questions, including the less logical ones, in a most logical to least logical fashion, he also enjoys working with architecture, research, analysis, development, testing, and bug fixing. Carsten is a very good communicator with great mentoring and team-lead skills and great skills researching and presenting new material.

Acknowledgments

Thank you Joshua Grimaud for your contributions to Chapter 9. Without your expertise, the chapter could not have been completed. Josh is an expert in programming and specifically DevSecOps. He is a creative thinker and a solution-oriented person. Also, he is a great friend and has an extreme passion for learning tech and creating music.

Introduction

This book was written to introduce the Microsoft Orleans framework and to provide an understanding of why it was created and how it can advance your current and potential applications. Actor model frameworks are not widely taught or known in mainstream development. Since the frameworks are not common knowledge, this book was written with beginners and intermediate developers in mind. An overview of Orleans is provided concerning topics such as how it can enhance projects, and how to get started in the code base.

First, we cover the origins of Orleans which was established in 2010. This book explains what it was built to accomplish and examples that showcase its successes in production. Next, we look at how Orleans works concerting lifecycles, which removes a massive amount of overhead from developers. Lifecycles are emphasized since they play a significant role in what makes Orleans unique by abstracting the work from the developers and making projects faster and more maintainable, compared with previous actor model frameworks. Next, we dive into commonly used architectures – monolithic and microservices – to show how Orleans can possibly enhance them. New and existing developers can benefit by learning how Orleans can extend their monolithic or microservice patterns.

The remainder of this book is hands-on coding where we set up a project and walk through adding features to it such as

- Timers and reminders

- Unit tests

- Dashboard

Then we walk through deploying Orleans to AKS. What good is our work if we cannot deploy for others to use it? I believe that all development books should have a deployment section so that the applications can be treated as real work. It allows you to deploy as we would in a business. We walk the setup of an app, code it, and deploy it. The pipeline will trigger when there is a commit and deploy if it meets the standards.

Finally, we conclude by summarizing what we have covered. We discuss where you can go next to further your journey with Orleans. I would treat this book as a strong starting point. It provides a strong understanding of what Orleans can do for you, how coding differs, resource requirements, and next steps.

## CHAPTER 1

A Primer on Microsoft Orleans and the Actor Model

Origins of Orleans

Microsoft Orleans is an open source project, which provides the developer with a simple programming model enabling them to build software, which can scale from a single machine to hundreds of servers.

You can think of Orleans as a distributed runtime, allowing the .NET developer to easily build software capable of processing high volumes of data and deployable to the cloud or on-premises.

Orleans is a "batteries included" framework, which ships with many of the features required for distributed systems built in.

First, what is an actor model? An actor model is defined as "a mathematical model of concurrent computation that treats 'actor' as the universal primitive of concurrent computation" (Patent Issued for Actor Model Programming (USPTO 10,768,902), 2020). Actor model frameworks use the model as a basis on which the frameworks pass messages between actors, and actors are created on a needed basis. Actor model frameworks are able to take advantage of concurrency through multicore computers and software abstraction. This means that actor model frameworks are able to process millions and billions of messages in real time or near-real time. We will cover this more in this chapter and throughout the book.

© Thomas Nelson 2022

T. Nelson, *Introducing Microsoft Orleans*, https://doi.org/10.1007/978-1-4842-8014-0_1

Orleans, created in 2010 by Microsoft Research, is an actor framework that harnesses the inert capabilities of cloud architecture (Orleans – Virtual Actors, 2018). The framework helps distribution experts and novices by using prebuilt libraries to create globally distributed, highly available, highly elastic robust solutions. The libraries remove many complexities –such as lifecycles – while using a common programming language. Ultimately, Orleans allows a single developer to create an extremely scalable application without being an expert in distributed system development. Other actor model frameworks require the developer to determine how to handle the life span of each actor and monitor and check health. Also, Orleans is a production-proven – through the use of IoT applications and game studios – and open source framework for Microsoft's internal and external flagship applications.

Origins and Use Cases of Orleans

Initially, Orleans was created to help expand cloud computing to a larger developer audience when cloud computing was new and gaining momentum. Orleans has the ability to provide hyper-scalable interactive services that support high throughput and availability with low latency in the cloud and local systems. Existing actor frameworks fulfill the technical needs; however, the additional overhead of knowledge, experience, and complex initial coding can be challenging to accomplish. Attempting to satisfy these requirements with a traditional three-tier service design is challenging as well. Orleans combines the common coding structures of three-tier development and .NET Core libraries, reducing entry barriers.

In addition to cloud development, it has been used for backend development of video games, such as the blockbusters *Halo 4, 5* and *Gears of War 4*. Cloud computing is extremely helpful in hosting and running distributed services for a global audience, such as gaming. Before cloud computing, the World Wide Web grew from its infancy, where servers were not readily globally distributed for businesses' applications, and clients accepted latency as a part of the Internet. I recall waiting for images to download a row or two at a time when using a 33.6k dial-up modem. Overtime, companies have risen to global entities, and cloud architecture creates the ability to cater to these clients in a distributed and real-time-like capacity. These changes lead to several new patterns emerging based on lessons learned, leading to Orleans' creation. To understand this process, we will discuss the development of services in a high-level perspective where we cover monolithic services, microservices, and Orleans.

Initially, monolithic applications were used to conduct multiple scopes of work. For instance, an application may house business logic server items, such as account, order, and shipping. Housing these together is necessarily a bad option, as each item depends on a single team. It allows the ability to walk through a single application for debugging and traceability. Unfortunately, this ability is associated with cons as well.

Monolithic applications have a large footprint. Since their scope maintains several items in the business, it is likely supported by several teams. Housing multiple large workflows together, a single application can get large and possibly unmaintainable overtime, if it is not watched closely. The larger the application, the more hardware it will require to support it, which can be costly in hosting hardware and perhaps startup time when needed on demand by consumers.

The application is usually tightly coupled and requires the teams to work and maintain open communication. This can hinder deployment as it is difficult, if not impossible, to deploy without all of the items being implemented. Feature flags can toggle various logic. However, strict discipline is required for the teams to stay within scope and communicate the changes internally; otherwise, it will delay deployment until all the work has been completed.

Overtime, *microservices* – a term coined by Dr. Peter Rogers – emerged to create granularly scoped applications that interact with one another to complete a holistic action(s). *Microservice* is a general term that refers to the scope of work of the application that is loosely coupled and generally uses standards such as REST, XML, JSON, and HTTP. Based on the preceding monolithic example, each logically scoped item that we mentioned – account, order, and shipping – is separated into its own service. Decoupling removes the need for multiple teams to maintain a single application and reduces complexity, thus facilitating communication and possibly on-time code completion to meet deployment deadlines. The footprints are a portion of what we would use for monolithic applications, which leads to the ability to scale out on demand.

Also, decoupling allows complex and extensive systems to be built, tested, and deployed individually. This adds value in an Minimal Viable Product (MVP) manner by being able to proceed with testing and deployment before the entire application completed whereas, the legacy application cannot move forward until all of the dependent work has been completed. Feature flags can be implemented however, the teams need to implement and maintain. When we refer to microservices in further chapters, we will be referring to a three-tier architecture (client, back end, database).

I have worked with monolithic services and microservices in several companies. I have gone through several transformation processes of converting monolithic applications to microservices. Microservice patterns are a solid choice for many of the current business needs and are supported easily by cloud computing. Cloud computing monitors the applications on set triggers to determine health and the need for scaling, among additional items.

I have moved between companies that had engineering teams of 40 to a few hundred to thousands. Each move to a larger company solidified --to me-- the need for maintainable services as cross-team communication was harder to sustain. This was/is due to members constantly moving or leaving within the teams, which removed the oversight and communication needed to maintain larger, monolithic applications. Again, this depends on the company structure, as the smaller teams made monolithic applications acceptable to work within.

This book will not debate the legitimacy of microservice vs. monolithic architectures but will discuss how the Orleans implementation can enhance applications and when Orleans is a good fit. Ultimately, the application needs and company structure should determine the design and technology that are chosen. The common goal of applications is to be a robust, extensible, and available system for consumers. For instance, a project might be required to implement a cloud hosting's concurrency and distribution as well as its dynamic and interactive in nature, which allows actor frameworks to flourish (Bernstein. P., Bykov, S.). Orleans was created, in part, to take advantage of these native cloud architecture abilities. The solution should be a negotiation between company ability and consumer needs.

To take full advantage of cloud computing, we can use Orleans, which is a production-ready – and battle-tested by supporting projects, like AAA video games and smart home IoT devices – framework written in C# and .NET Core and distributed in NuGet (New Get) packages with version 2.0+, which creates cloud-agnostic solutions. This allows .NET developers to extend their applications within an already familiar ecosystem. Orchestration overhead is reduced through the framework's ability to maintain lifecycles and elasticity and harness the actor model's concurrency. The actor model uses actors, which are fine-grained isolated objects that receive and send asynchronous messages with the ability to create additional actors (Bernstein & Bykov, 2016).

Actor frameworks can be complicated for developers to understand since they can be complex and are not commonly taught in universities. It usually takes a team or teams of advanced engineers to create and maintain a system. Orleans came into existence to help reduce the overhead and barriers and take advantage of the actor model's capabilities. In 2015, Microsoft chose to open-source Orleans, which resulted in a large community where Microsoft continues to accept contributions. The framework's community support displays that Orleans is the/a viable solution that solves the gap when creating distributed, elastic, cloud-agnostic, and maintainable services.

Essentially, Orleans harnesses the cloud's (Azure, AWS, GCP) geo-decentralized nature and reduces traditional actor framework overheads, such as developing and maintaining Akka and Erlang actors' lifecycle. Instead, Orleans allows a single developer, without in-depth actor knowledge, to create globally decentralized applications rather than requiring a specialized actor team. Also, the framework reduces the overall learning curve for non–actor model developers to get started and build actor model applications.

Orleans is a cluster what can thought of a monolithic service yet, decoupled like microservices. Therefore, it is essential to understand the differences in the architectures and why using Orleans can benefit your architectures. Actor frameworks are based on the mathematical actor model.

Actor Model Explained

The term *actor model* can be defined for our purposes as a true concept of concurrency in an abstract application created in 1973 by Carl Hewitt (Clebsch et al., 2019). In a nutshell, it uses an application as the abstraction from the processor and has actors that pass async messages for concurrency. Actors perform work within three functions:

1. Defined communications for other actors.

2. Logic is performed on the message before passing it to the next actor.

3. There are a fixed number of new actors created (Gul Agha).

To summarize, each actor knows how to handle the work sent to it and where the message will be passed next and can create actors. Thus, we can think of an actor as a micro-application/function that accepts a message, performs some sort of logic based on the message, and is either the terminal actor or passes a message to another actor.

Actors communicate through messages and queues. As seen in Figure 1-1, each actor has its queue, processes its messages, and passes them to the next actor's mailbox. It is a common practice to process a single message at a time. The actors are in an isolated state, which means they do not need to share access so that if a single actor instance fails, it will not affect the other instances. Once the logic has been completed, the actor will asynchronously pass the message to the newly created/existing actor's queue. Each actor is uniquely defined by means such as Globally Unique Identities (GUIDs), paths, and Uniform Resource Identifiers (URIs).

The messaging delivery guarantee determines message delivery reliability. There are three types of messaging guarantees that vary in resource expense:

1. *At-Most-Once* – The message will be delivered zero or one time, which means that the message may be lost. This is what Orleans implements. A message will never be delivered twice, but it will be delivered once or not at all (Microsoft, n.d.).

2. *At-Least-Once* – Multiple attempts of the message are made for delivery.

3. *Exactly-Once* – A single message will be delivered once, which also has the most considerable amount of overhead.

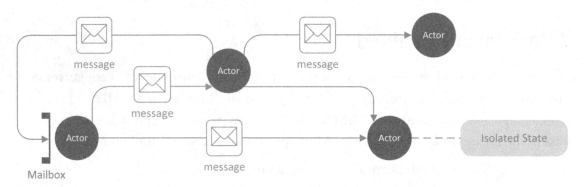

Figure 1-1. *Actor model message flow. Each actor runs in an isolated state and passes messages to the receiving actor's mailbox until the work has been completed (modified from Mankevich, 2013)*

A single actor can complete the entire job alone or send it to another actor to complete the work. It depends on the architectural design and implementation. The additional actor can be called to process a specific scope of work, much like microservices. For instance, actors can easily maintain billions and even trillions of concurrent transactions on a global network. Actor frameworks are commonly associated with Internet of Things (IoT) development, Artificial Intelligence (AI), and game development. They can be thought of as a class or a few code classes containing business logic. It creates a feature-rich mesh network of tools. The tiny objects also support AI development solutions by mimicking neurons that work based on logic across billions of nodes to create an overall objective.

Actor Model Infused with Orleans

Orleans was built on the actor model's qualities by maintaining the granular aspect, queues, asynchronicity, and concurrency. Project Orleans reduces the overhead by managing the lifecycle of actors, referred to as virtual actors or grains within the Orleans framework, that frameworks such as Akka and Erlang require the developers to maintain. Lifecycles are tedious work for developers due to setting up the activation, waiting between jobs, and knowing when to deactivate the actor. At the same time, a new actor is initiated or overextends its time, which hordes resources. Both instances can be detrimental or, in some cases, catastrophic, which is why expert distributed programmers generally build and support these systems.

Orleans reduces the low-level coding requirements by implementing the grain lifecycle into the framework. Without this overhead, it is easier for developers to implement the business logic faster. The addition of grain the grain lifecycle allows a single developer to create and maintain applications, while errors have significantly reduced risk based on framework management.

The messaging delivery guarantee for Orleans is at-most-once by default. This means that messages can be lost, although an acknowledgment message is returned when a message is delivered.

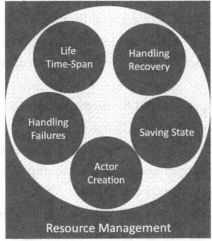
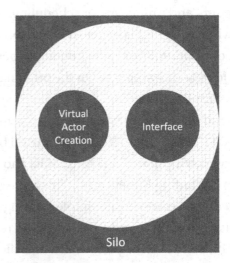

Figure 1-2. *Actors vs. virtual actors concerning low-level complexity. Developers manually create the actors' common low-level complexities, whereas the Orleans framework supports or handles the complexities by default*

Orleans creates and maintains the "actors" in memory. To differentiate Orleans' actors from traditional actors, we refer to them as virtual actors or grains, as we can see in Figure 1-2. We use the same naming reference to distinguish between conventional actors and those of Orleans. Silos manage the grains.

Silos are distributed resource management applications that sit between clients and grains and perform grain checks to secure reliability. Multiple silos can run and communicate with one another in a cluster. The silo can create grains or send messages to already active grains on behalf of the client's request. Also, they monitor grains' health, and in the event of a grain failing, deactivation, or garbage collection, a silo may need to restart, or new grains will need to be initialized. Silos can also request grains through other silos that can share communications, such as exceptions.

The grains can also share atomic, consistent, isolated, and durable (ACID) transactions. The transactions have Serializable Isolation – which is the most isolated of the standard transaction levels. Also, lock-based concurrency controls remove write collisions. Orleans transactions do not use a centralized transaction manager, which would limit performance and scalability.

Also, grains support managed streams and timed triggers. The streams are an abstraction for a wide range of queuing systems. They also support batching with queues and checkpoints. The checkpoints allow the stream to be aware of the last items removed to maintain sending the correct subsequent item in the line. Clouds such as Azure, AWS, and GCP can connect to Orleans through queueing mechanisms and stream providers. Reminders and timers are for scheduling. Reminders are durable, which can be used even when the grain is not currently active. However, timers are nondurable and can be used for one-offs or more frequent repetition. For example, a reminder can trigger batch jobs or daily reports. On the other hand, timers can start periodic health checks of various applications.

Cloud agnosticism is an up-and-coming staple in current development designs, which .NET Core and .NET 6 and beyond help facilitate. Since Orleans uses these frameworks, it can run on Linux, Mac, and Windows machines, both on-premises and in clouds (including Kubernetes). This removed the barrier and removed the dependency on selecting a cloud host or implementing the multi-cloud architecture.

It is important to note that interfaces reference all grains to maintain decoupling based on SOLID principles. Grains and silos call one another based on interfaces that inherit decoupling and prime the stage for unit testing. This creates a choice of architecture regarding how you would like to share the Orleans backend applications with clients. The interfaces can be embedded within the client application, or a proxy client can be established, allowing other clients to call endpoints of the proxy client without being coupled to grains' interfaces.

Note: SOLID principles were created for object-oriented programming languages to define good coding practices that help with items such as future maintenance.

S – Single responsibility, where a class should only have a single responsibility and a single reason for the change, which vigorously enforces the class's scope.

O – Open-closed, where classes should only be open for extension and closed to modification, which is to deter previously added code changes that increase error risk.

L – Liskov substitution allows us to swap classes with their subclasses, such as having a base class and using its subclasses.

I – Interface segregation consists of breaking more extensive interfaces into smaller ones in that they are only focused on methods used.

D – Dependency inversion decouples classes by basing the class outlines on abstracts, allowing multiple classes to be used in their stead. (Oloruntoba, 2020)

Grain Lifecycle

Orleans implements automated lifecycles for grains. This greatly reduces the overhead on developers and makes implementing an actor framework much more straightforward. This is one of the aspects that makes Orleans developer-friendly and very powerful out of the box. Many other abilities are offered, and we will cover them throughout the book; however, a grain lifecycle is an effective tool that simplifies how one takes advantage of distributed frameworks.

Other actor frameworks, such as Akka, are dependent on the developers to write code to activate and dispose of the instances. That means that we would need to program the time for each actor to live once the job has been completed. Also, there will need to be a way to determine if the actor instance is active or it will need to be created to send it a message. It is up to us to determine how these items are handled. It may not seem like a lot of work; however, as actors are added and needs vary, it can become a significant task.

Single Developer

As mentioned, Orleans removes a significant amount of overhead for developers to the extent that a single developer can create each portion of the solution. Also, it allows the developer to set up the application quickly. This allows setup to be minimized, and value can be added in the shorter term by focusing on business logic.

For instance, if we create the same project in Erlang as we do in Orleans, Erlang will require more preparation time than Orleans. This is because the Erlang application will need to be thoughtfully prepared before building the structural items, such as actor time spans, and implement the base-level code before implementing business logic. On the other hand, Orleans has these items baked into the framework and allows developers to configure them as needed. The pre-baked items will enable the developer to quickly set up the base projects and begin development sooner.

The atomicity of grains and decoupling allow maintenance and extensibility to be easily added. This pattern has been popular due to SOLID principles where applications are built-in modular, encapsulated classes that will enable promoting extensibility. Grains naturally fit within these patterns based on size and by maintaining state. In addition, grain logic's scoped boundaries and running on a single thread allow for simple additions for extending and updating logic.

Adding features is as easy as building interfaces, creating the grain(s) logic, and updating existing grains. The framework makes a straightforward way for developers to add and modify items as needed. Also, it allows multiple developers to work on separate grains at the same time. This allows extending the mesh network as the business grows logically and a phased approach as needed, commonly handled with microservice development teams.

A grain uses the following interface:

```
namespace ChapterOneExample.Interfaces
{
    public interface IChapterOne : Orleans.IGrainWithStringKey
    {
        Task<string> ReturnMessage(string greeting);
    }
}
```

There are several interface keys we can use to differentiate the grain instances. It depends on the use case of the application to determine which.

In this case, we are using IGrainWithStringKey, which differentiates the grain's instance identity by a string name. The choices are:

- IGrainWithGuidCompoundKey – <GUID + string>

  - Example: e1254329-ea06-427f-a097-8343a07d29a1TestGrain

- IGrainWithGuidKey – <GUID>

  - Example: e1254329-ea06-427f-a097-8343a07d29a1

- IGrainWithIntegerCompoundKey – <long + string>

  - Example: 123546TestGrain

- IGrainWithIntegerKey – <long>

  - Example: 123456

- IGrainWithStringKey – <string>

  - Example: TestGrain

A grain is easily added, as seen in the following:

```
namespace ChapterOneExample.Grains
{
    public class ChapterOne : Orleans.Grain, IChapterOne
    {
        Task<string> IChapterOne.ReturnMessage(string message)
        {
            logger.LogInformation($"Message: {message}");
            return Task.FromResult($"Sent message: {message}");
        }
    }
}
```

Chapter 5 will cover the initial setup of the grains, interfaces, silo, and client; however, understand that the silo and client are set up and send requests to the grains. The client will send a request in the following example:

```
private static async Task SendMessage(IClusterClient client)
        {

                var chapter1Example = client.GetGrain<IChapterOne>("TestGrain");
                var response = await chapter1Example.ReturnMessage("Message
                From Client");

        }
```

The preceding example displays the ease of adding features and how easily they are consumed. Also, this example displays the separation of logic, which allows developers to work in separate sections in parallel.

Production Uses and History

Orleans – since its creation in 2010 – has proven its reliability in production environments. Writing this book has aged nearly a decade, although not widely known or marketed to the public. A few of the projects that Orleans has supported or supports include (Who Is Using Orleans? | Microsoft Orleans website, n.d.):

- *Microsoft Skype* – Instant messaging

- *Honeywell Devices* – Internet of Things

- *Microsoft Halo 4* – Player statistics, health checks, lobbies

These applications all share common scenarios where the transactions are small and need to work together to produce an overarching product that requires concurrency. For instance, instant messaging may require billions/trillions of parallel transactions that are burstable.

Honeywell devices would work in the same manner. Each device signals changes in state, and the application might calculate outcomes/actions based on the signals. For instance, the weather may affect the house's temperature; however, only the room with activity needs to be heated. Also, movement may trigger lights to turn on; yet, a cooldown may not have been met, which would then not trigger the event, as it would be too soon.

Halo uses Orleans which has proven how well the framework performs under extreme utilization. Real-time statistics of each player were needed to be tracked. This was easily obtained through the distributed concurrency and high throughput of Orleans by scaling up memory and processors. The results were remarkable as it did not fail when running a constant 90% load and expanded from 25 to 125 servers (Bernstein & Bykov, 2016). The application would support matchmaking, player statistics, and individual health checks. The servers scaled to a maximum of 125 servers to support the needs of the video game *Halo*; however, it did not determine the maximum amount of scaling supported by Orleans. Orleans could scale further if it was required (Bernstein & Bykov, 2016).

Based on the examples, it is clear that the framework is stable, maintainable, and proven by companies relying on it to support projects. Orleans has been used in projects in some form by the following companies (Who Is Using Orleans? | Microsoft Orleans website, n.d.):

- Gassumo

- Microsoft

- Microsoft Studios

- Microsoft Research

- NašeÚkoly.CZ

- Trustev

- Mailcloud Limited

- Gigya

- Honeywell

- Mesh Systems

- Applicita Limited

- Drawboard

- YouScan

- Visa

How does this relate to us since these are substantial companies with an army of developers? Orleans allows a single developer to build the system. It is more cost-efficient to create a start with an extendable design or framework. It doesn't matter if you are working for a startup or a small to large business or freelancing; Orleans allows us to start from a strong foundation and grow. Also, applications can be redesigned and refactored into Orleans. It is essential to understand that the application's needs determine the tools required, which is discussed in Chapter 4.

Summary

In this chapter, we discussed the origins of Orleans, which was created in 2011 by Microsoft Research and proven with game development and IoT. It was created for cloud development by providing highly-scalable interactive services that supports high throughput and availability with the infusion of low latency based on the principles of the actor model. The low-level development burden on the engineers is removed along with a large portion of the learning curve for engineers. Experts can tackle business cases sooner.

The actor model was created for real-time concurrency. Each actor is tiny and has a mailbox. The actor model is based on three rules:

1. Defined communications for other actors

2. Some form of logic on the message before passing it to the next actor

3. Fixed number of new actors created

   (Agha, 1986).

Actors have three levels of guarantees that are related to message delivery:

1. *At-Most-Once* – The message will be delivered zero or one time, which means that the message may be lost.

2. *At-Least-Once* – The message will be recreated multiple times to be delivered.

3. *Exactly-Once* – A single message is created and will not be lost, which also has the most considerable amount of overhead.

14

We also discussed how Orleans naturally supports the SOLID principles by requiring interfaces that decouple classes while single-threaded grains force classes to be highly focused and maintainable.

The grain lifecycle makes developing much easier than that of other actor frameworks. It doesn't force the developer to determine the lifespan and monitoring of each grain. It is handled automatically by the framework and can be adjusted as needed.

Production uses of Orleans have proven its robustness and its extreme value. It has been established in high-end game development with *Halo 4 and 5* and *Gears of War 4*. When tested with *Halo 4*, it expanded to 125 servers while running over 90% utilization without errors. Honeywell has also utilized the framework for its IoT devices, a backbone feature for many of its products.

In the next chapter, we will dive further into Orleans and how items work together. We will also discuss common uses of fabric frameworks and standard features that are available for implementation.

CHAPTER 2

Introducing Microsoft Orleans

What Can Orleans Do for Us?

Orleans helps developers to easily create cloud-native, elastic, highly available applications. It allows us to take advantage of the actor framework attributes such as elasticity, concurrency, and high availability without having to be an expert in distributed systems. Services such as IoT, Stock exchanges, and email systems are great use cases for actor frameworks. What is truly amazing about it is that it gives a single dev the ability to write an application themselves by using a few NuGet packages, common failure practices, and Orleans' coding guidelines.

In this chapter we will discuss commonly used projects where the actor framework was used and why. Then we will cover Orleans' base packages, community support, and supported technologies.

Cloud-Native, Elastic, Highly Available

The distributed and concurrent characteristics of actor frameworks take advantage of cloud computing architecture (Bernstein & Bykov, 2016). Orleans can be connected to many resources that expand its multi-cloud development support. High elasticity and availability characteristics result from several factors based on the granular-sized objects in collaboration with the framework's ability to monitor and maintain the clusters.

© Thomas Nelson 2022
T. Nelson, *Introducing Microsoft Orleans*, https://doi.org/10.1007/978-1-4842-8014-0_2

Elasticity and availability are primarily due to:

- Grain size

  - Grains are not restricted to size; however, they are not generally built on a monolithic scale and do not implement items like the startup information like required in microservices. Grains are straight to business logic, without the fluff. This supports a fast activations, especially since they live within the runtime.

- Health monitoring

  - Silos monitor each other's health within a cluster.

- Lifecycles

  - Intelligent orchestration of lifecycles permits the likelihood of resources to be available when grains need to be created.

Using Orleans can negate the need for additional platform tools – such as caching and API management. The clusters/silos are commonly deployed to Kubernetes, which simplifies deployment and resource availability rather than manually maintaining VMs. Silos and grains are readily available without network changes, such as firewalls and application management. These can be achieved without having to rely on third-party tools and balancing multiple runtimes. However, Orleans does commit us to .NET Core/.NET and Orleans' framework, whereas microservices allow us the flexibility of writing them in any language and third-party tools. It is important to weigh these options based on the requirements and future needs of the application(s).

Common Use Cases for Actor Model Frameworks

In the previous chapter, we reviewed Orleans composed projects to showcase its robustness through previous implementations from highly successful organizations. However, a project doesn't need to be as large and complex as the examples in order to implement Orleans. The point is that we don't need to work on an enterprise stock market application to consider Orleans as a possible solution.

Tools are selected based on the business objectives, growth, and client interactivity (including latency thresholds and APIs) required of the project. A common rule of thumb is that if items are expected to scale beyond a single server, be highly concurrent, and be elastic, then Orleans might be a correct fit (Microsoft, n.d.). Many applications can be broken down from microservices into virtual actors; however, not every application needs to be broken into grains.

Technically, the items that correlate with Orleans projects are as follows (Microsoft, n.d.):

- Hundreds or even trillions of objects that are loosely coupled.

- Atomic entities that can run in in a single thread.

- Interactive activities, such as responses and requests.

- The requirement of or growth to more than one server.

- Holistic management is not required as grains maintain their tasks.

To provide further understanding, examples such as the following meet the requirements:

- *Internet of Things* – Billions/trillions of signals from devices communicate with the cluster, which triggers various events such as a change in temperature. Maintaining individual transactions on a global scale requires harmonization of the application, high concurrency, and high elasticity. IoT is one of the most commonly used examples for actor model frameworks due to each grain representing each device. IoT is decentralized, and concurrency is required with consistent transactions from every active device.

- *Instant Messaging* – A vast number of transactions are needed to be orchestrated to the correct parties which could span across the globe.This is easily handled by Orleans since grains can represent each party member and speak to clusters in other regions. This is explained in further chapters.

- *Gaming* – Game lobbies and statistics need to be incredibly elastic and decentralized due to players living around the world. They are also required to maintain unique games types, characters, player lobbies, etc. groups for multiplayer type games. Also, each player's information of kills, deaths, etc. must be recorded in real time and tallied against the leaderboard.

- *Reservations* – Based on the project's scale, reservations will have to be tracked and locked as they are accepted. Elasticity, decentralization, and concurrency are required during times of high demand. For instance, airline/hotel reservations are in more increased need during holidays, and a sudden fluctuation of users should not impact clients. The clients can make reservations from anywhere globally, and when a reservation is filled, this needs to be locked without double booking. The ability of virtual actors to communicate with one another and databases solves this issue.

- *Stock Exchange* – The stock exchange requires concurrency and elasticity, which calculates prices based on demand and tracking stocks' sales. A significant amount of elasticity is required for availability during peak trading times. Concurrency will also be essential to maintain a steady flow of accurate trading statistics derived from the trades.

- *Gambling* – Like the stock exchange, bets can be placed from any location, which requires availability. Before games and races, placed bets are prone to significantly increase in a short amount of time. Each bet needs to be stored and associated with each user for possible payouts and amounts.

- *Telecommunications* – Telecom companies must create massively scalable and concurrent systems that allow node, tower, and service-switching flexibility.

- *Email* – A scalable and robust solution that can decipher multiple protocols is a foundational enterprise-capable pillar.

Microsoft Orleans Base Libraries, Community, and Included Technologies

Create and Maintain an Orleans Application as a Single Developer

As mentioned, by creating virtual actors that have maintained lifecycles, a significant amount of overhead has been removed from the developers. We want to highlight the simplicity-to-value ratio that can be produced by utilizing the framework. We will accomplish this by walking through the creation of a base application. Then we will build this base by adding features.

Setting up a project is a straightforward and repeatable process. The client, interfaces, grains, and silo will need to be created, as well as importing the NuGet packages with the correct project. The libraries are built in .NET Core and constantly updated to the latest .NET Core version to take advantage of the framework and to have the ability to be ported into non-Windows environments.

Additional information regarding Orleans' NuGet packages can be found here: `https://dotnet.github.io/orleans/docs/tutorials_and_samples/tutorial_1.html`.

When starting with a new project, the items are set up in a single solution and contain the packages list in Table 2-1, which makes developing and debugging straightforward. Microsoft was kind enough to create templates for the silo and client to get any project started. The base templates can be found here: `https://dotnet.github.io/orleans/docs/tutorials_and_samples/tutorial_1.html`.

Table 2-1. *Orleans base NuGet packages. These are the base packages and their associated projects. Each Orleans project will incorporate these packages and projects:*

Project	NuGet Package
Silo	Microsoft.Orleans.Server
	Microsoft.Extensions.Logging.Console
Client	Microsoft.Extensions.Logging.Console
	Microsoft.Orleans.Client
Grain interfaces	Microsoft.Orleans.Core.Abstractions
	Microsoft.Orleans.CodeGenerator.MSBuild
Grains	Microsoft.Orleans.CodeGenerator.MSBuild
	Microsoft.Orleans.Core.Abstractions
	Microsoft.Extensions.Logging.Abstractions

Once the initial silo is set up and tested, we are ready to start customizing the solution for our needs. That's it! After that point, we would determine storage locations and begin development. Storage locations can be set in memory for development until a permanent solution is available on-premises or in a cloud. Additional features can be included in a modular format through updating grains or adding additional ones.

Community and Constant Advancements

Orleans has wonderful communities for both new and veteran developers. Based on the type of communication and the form of information you are looking to obtain, there are several choices:

Twitter – Twitter is used for general updates and version releases. They can be found @msftorleans. Videos, such as Channel9 developer interviews, are tagged as well.

Gitter – Gitter is an online developer community. The Orleans team is in the transition to leave Gitter and move to Discord with the same wonderful support. Developers of applications, such as Microsoft Orleans, use this platform to communicate and work with developers –both inside and outside of Microsoft – working with their tools. It also supports open source development where developers can help with tooling by writing extensions, documentation, or answering questions. Orleans' documentation, which is stored on Orleans' GitHub forum, can be located at `https://gitter.im/dotnet/orleans`. Here, you will find a very supportive community that will help beginners and veterans.

Discord – Discord has primarily been used by gamers due to its ease of use, easy voice calls, messaging channels, and authorization allowances. The Orleans team and supports are moving to Discord and away from Gitter. The Discord server is `https://aka.ms/orleans-discord`.

LinkedIn – LinkedIn is used to network workers and companies. As a part of this offering, groups were added to support knowledge growth. The official LinkedIn Orleans group can be found at `www.linkedin.com/groups/12276020/`. The same developers who can be found on Gitter are on LinkedIn; however, the Gitter community is more active.

GitHub – Orleans' documentation and examples are stored in GitHub. The published documentation is available here: `https://dotnet.github.io/orleans/`. Microsoft recently started adding documentation concerning Orleans here: `https://docs.microsoft.com/en-us/dotnet/orleans`.

Anyone, including yourself, can contribute to Orleans through the Community Contributions repo: `https://github.com/OrleansContrib/`. Anyone can add project examples and add to or modify the documentation. The Microsoft team will review, possibly add comments to, and merge the branch, if it meets the team's quality standards. Additional contribution guidelines can be found here: `https://dotnet.github.io/orleans/docs/resources/contributing.html`.

Multiple Hosting Solutions Are Supported

The framework can execute locally, on-premises, and in any cloud that supports .NET Core/.NET. It is commonly deployed to Kubernetes, readily available in the common cloud hosting platforms – AWS, GCP, and Azure. Orleans can be deployed with or without containers. This gives the ability to deploy to Docker Swarm or Kubernetes and opens up a large selection of hosting platforms, including on-premises or in the cloud.

The release of Orleans 2.0 changed the distribution from templates into NuGet packages. Before version 2.0, Visual Studio templates were required to build Orleans projects and are only available in the .NET Framework. Switching to NuGet packages allows DevOps practices to be applied to the distributing releases in a uniform and version-controlled manner. Doing so enables CI/CD pipelines with feeds to treat Orleans applications similar to microservices. While completing this book Orleans version 4 preview was made available that includes major logging enhancements, grain identity improvements, and a version-fault tolerant serializer. More on this tolpic cna be found here: `https://github.com/dotnet/orleans/releases/tag/v4.0.0-preview1`. Also, Orleans is consistently being updated to take advantages of the latest .NET versions, such as .NET 7. The Orleans' roadmap for .NET 7 can be found here: `https://github.com/dotnet/aspnetcore/issues/39504`.

Resource Management and Expansion

Orleans lifecycle manages resources by activating and deactivating grains. In comparison, when transactions are flooding an application, whether it be a monolithic or a microservice, the ability to scale remains the same. When horizontal scaling, the creation of additional application instances requires additional resource allocation to support each instance. Both monolithic and microservice applications are scaled based on various triggers, such as CPU usage, which creates an additional instance of the entire application even though the entire application's logic is not being used. Grains are maintained by the Orleans' runtime and are likely smaller than monolithic apps where, like microservices are smaller and reduce overhead on an individual basis. The runtime takes care of the activation process and greatly reduces the "going live" process with apps on the could. When I worked and a developer, scaling microservices could be seen taking ~30 seconds up to ~3 minutes whereas, grains are seen as always being active, thanks to the runtime. Since grains can accept work at anytime, means that the grain's state will not matter or be noticed by the user.

For instance, if a single endpoint receives enough transactions that trigger a scale-out event, the entire application will be instantiated, even though only a portion is being utilized. Instead, Orleans' grains are activated and deactivated when requested. Suppose the silo is receiving increased traffic, just as the service in the preceding example. Only the grains correlated with the work will be created and automatically deactivated. This ability allows for more efficient usage of resources, enabling more transactions and reducing costs. Chapter 4 will cover this in detail, where we will review monolithic, microservice applications and their abilities and how an Orleans backend might enhance them.

Clusters can expand by scaling up a resource, such as memory and processors. Cloud platforms remove the overhead of having to add resources to the servers through automated scaling. Orleans grain orchestration allows the developer to not have to determine horizontal scaling since the grain instances are handed by the runtime. Clouds make vertical scaling easy implement, which works wonderfully with Orleans applications as resource needs fluctuate.

Failure Handling

Clouds are built with commodity hardware, and your software is hosted in a shared environment where resources such as the network are highly contended. Failure is common, both in the form of total node loss and transient network outages. Software running in the cloud must be able to handle failures.

A majority of error handling rests in developers' hands, just as it is with on-prem applications. Orleans takes care of the heavy lifting with health monitoring and fault tolerance. Traditional troubleshooting techniques and tools to mitigate or correct failures are listed below:

- Implement a retry, which can be easily accomplished by using a tool such as Polly, which can be found here: `www.polly.ai/`.

- Attempt to correct or resend the object so that it reverts to the last known healthy state before continuing the workflow.

- Reset the state of the transaction and rerun the transaction from the beginning of the workflow.

- Implement a retry that sends unchanged messages to compensate for message delivery failure. Code can be added to determine if it is a duplicate and disregard it if required.

Additional information can be found here: `https://dotnet.github.io/orleans/docs/deployment/handling_failures.html`.

Streaming

Orleans streaming allows "fine-grained free-form compute over stream data" (Why Orleans Streams? | Microsoft Orleans Documentation, n.d.), which current systems do not support. Each data item can be treated differently and even allows external calls to be made. In current systems, "unified data-flow graph of operations that are applied in the same way to all stream items" rather on an individual basis (Why Orleans Streams? | Microsoft Orleans Documentation, n.d.). Orleans can extend streams such as Kafka, EventHub, Apache Spark, Apache Storm, and Azure Stream Analytics to have more individual control when needed.

Streaming is supported; however, granularity differs from the current streaming frameworks, such as Kafka. Current systems stream unified information rather than being seen on an individual basis. Orleans streams allows the ability for each streamed grain to connect with a specific destination.

Orleans streaming follows these requirements:

1. *Flexible Streams* – Orleans gives us the power to choose how to set up the stream. We can write the data-flow, by using Reactive Extensions (Rx), functional, or imperial logic based on our needs and team background (Microsoft, n.d.).

2. *Dynamic Topologies* – Topologies are not static and can be changed during runtime, whereas other existing streaming technology are not as dynamic.

3. Fine Grained Stream Grainularity – Orleans' streams are an abstraction based on existing streaming technologies, such as Kafka (Microsoft, n.d.). Orleans allows us to manage per grains in the stream, rather than the unified approach.

4. *Distribution* – It supports a large amount of streams, elasticity, quick recovery from failures, efficient resource usage, and virtual real-time responsiveness (Microsoft, n.d.).

Additional information can be found here: `https://dotnet.github.io/orleans/docs/streaming/streams_why.html`.

Persistence

Persistence pertains to storing information in a database. Orleans has a convenient persistence model that allows the state of the grain to be stored in a choice of backing stores, such as SQL, Azure Storage, and Amazon DynamoDB (Microsoft, n.d.). It collects the data while the grain is being activated. Each grain can have multiple data objects; however, it is noted that this is not a "silver bullet" to be used for all occasions. It was created to make it easier to connect to some database types and is not required for connection. The developer has a choice to either use the built-in persistence model or to specifically call the database through the grain without the use of the grain persistence model.

Having multiple abilities to save data allows flexibility in design, implementation, and options. Data objects show the ingenuity that the teams are building into the framework which reduces development overhead and latency. The Data objects are easily implemented and gather information during the grain activation state. This is a prime example of how the Orleans' team and its community attempt to handle Orleans' goals of developer support and framework optimization. Grains can also be used as caching object where they can store the latest results from the database and be queried prior to a database request. This is known as the Smart Caching pattern. Additional information regarding Smart Caching can be found here: `https://github.com/OrleansContrib/DesignPatterns/blob/master/Smart%20Cache.md`.

Summary

This chapter covered several common uses of Orleans/Actor framework services, such as stock exchange, gambling applications, telecommunications, and email servers. Each of these tools requires concurrency, interactivity, and scalability. Actor frameworks are not confined to these examples and are capable of handling many other business needs.

Orleans consists of base NuGet packages and projects. Each cluster consists of grain interfaces, a silo, grains, and a client. The client makes requests to the silo, based on grain interfaces, and the silo orchestrates the messages between the grains and the client. The silo also maintains resource allocation, which allows a single developer to write the entire Orleans service.

The flourishing community can help people learn Orleans, extend their knowledge, stay up to date, and support the open source framework. Twitter has general updates, version release announcements, and video recommendations. Gitter connects us to the developers working on Microsoft Orleans and other experts. It is a wonderful place to visit when you are stumped or stop in and say "Hi." The LinkedIn group connects additional people interested in Orleans and has a forum. GitHub houses the documentation and source code. This is where you can suggest code extensions and documentation updates through check-ins. There is documentation being stood up on Microsoft docs and the team live support is transitioning to discord.

Additional features are available in Orleans to extend abilities and remove additional burdens from the developer:

- Failure handling allows developers to handle errors, in the same manner with traditional three-tier architecture. Silos are able to communicate with one another to share errors as needed.

- Streaming can be combined with other streaming services such as Kafka. The primary difference is that Orleans allows a granular stream rather than Kafka streams, which is based on unified rather than granular streams.

- Persistence can be used by each grain. Orleans added Persistent Data Objects to data during the activation state. It is not required, but a helpful feature, as each grain can query a database through connection strings as well.

- Grain caching is set up in Orleans by storing values in another grain and calling it before a database call. This is a pattern known as smart caching, which provides the option of not using a third-party cache.

In the next chapter, we will discuss the lifecycles of grains and the silo. This will be a more in-depth look to understand the cycles and why Orleans works as it does.

CHAPTER 3

Lifecycles

In this chapter, we will cover the lifecycle of grains, a silo, transaction paths, and clusters. We discussed the grain lifecycle in Chapter 1, Figure 1-2, as a foundational pillar. The grain lifecycle was designed to reduce low-level work for the developer. The silo was constructed to host the grains and provide the runtime. Each transaction has a cycle, which is dependent on the work required. Silos also have a process that allows them to be added to and removed from clusters.

Grain Lifecycle

Automatically managing the lifecycle of grains, Orleans dramatically simplifies the development of distributed systems. Lifecycles were created to remove the low-level abstractions, which diminishes the overhead, barrier of learning, and risk of non-proper resource management for developers. In my opinion, it is a phenomenal advancement of actor model frameworks. It reduces barriers for developers to learn and implement an actor model principles while taking advantage of the actor model framework's abilities while working within NET. Complexity is greatly reduced and business logic is surprisingly placed well front-and-center with grains.

© Thomas Nelson 2022

T. Nelson, *Introducing Microsoft Orleans*, https://doi.org/10.1007/978-1-4842-8014-0_3

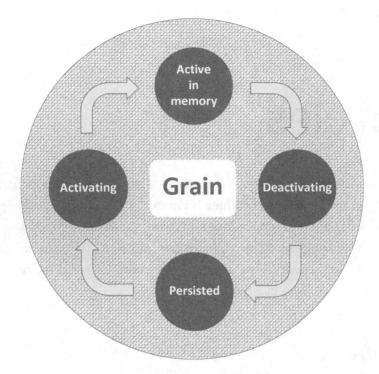

Figure 3-1. *Grain lifecycle. Orleans' framework maintains each grain's lifecycle. At any given time, a grain is in one of four states: activating, active, deactivating, and then persisted. It does not matter the current state of the grain as it can always be invoked with a request, and the request will be processed by the grain. The cycle consists of the grain being activated, becoming active, deactivating, and then being persisted for future use. Modified from "Orleans is a cross-platform framework for building robust, scalable distributed applications": Microsoft Orleans Documentation*

Here is the lifecycle as displayed in Figure 3-1 (modified from Microsoft):

1. *Activation* – Activation occurs when a request arrives for the grain that isn't currently active. This is where the grain instance is initialized in memory. For instance, when an action is requested, the silo will lazily activate the grain. The grain is initiated in memory. Once the grain is active, then requests can be worked. The grain will stay active based on the fulfillment of requests. It allows developers to code as if the grain if it always active (Microsoft, n.d.).

2. *Active in Memory* – All of the grains are active in memory. While fulfilling work, action logs will be persisted in the database of the developer's choice. The grain will be active in memory and is ready to accept work, even if there aren't any new requests. This was done as preparation to handle additional requests.

- If the grain is busy when requested, the message will be stored in a queue until the grain is ready.

- Turn-based concurrency keeps all subsequent tasks on the same thread as the grain that created them (Microsoft, n.d.). New tasks will all run on the same thread as the parent as per the TPL Task Scheduler. This means that only one execution is permitted and others are stuck in await to remove race conditions from parallel threads.

3. *Deactivation* – Once the grain stops receiving requests in a time period, then it will be sent to the deactivation state. This state is in preparation to be persisted in the database and removed from memory.

4. *Persisted* – The grain will be changed to a persisted state where its final state is stored to a database. This will free up resources for other grains and/or reduce resource needs, which lowers cloud costs. The grain is removed from memory and persisted in a database.

The cycle repeats when requests are made targeting the grain and if it was deactivated. The lifecycle is immensely powerful as is. It lets the application scale based on the real-time needs, rather than initializing additional applications, which waste resources, when a single execution flow is being utilized.

As supportive and helpful as the framework is for maintaining the lifecycles behind the scenes, developers may need to trigger events based on states. Observable lifecycle allows objects to be sequenced to start up and shut down based on triggers. Additionally, it allows objects to view the state of the lifecycle of another object. Additional information can be found here: Orleans Lifecycle | Microsoft Orleans Documentation (dotnet.github.io).

A silo's lifecycle is similar to a grain's lifecycle. Orleans' documentation breaks the silo lifecycle into the following steps (Microsoft, n.d.):

1. First stage in a service's lifecycle.

2. Initializes the runtime environment, and the silo initializes threading.

3. Runtime services are started, and the silo initializes various agents and networking.

4. Initializes runtime storage.

5. Starts runtime services for grains, which includes grain type management, membership service, and Grain Directory.

6. Application layer services.

7. The silo is joined to the cluster.

8. The silo is active in the cluster and ready to accept workload.

9. Last stage in a service's lifecycle.

Grain Reentrancy

Grains are marked as busy for the duration of a method call, even while they are awaiting external tasks. Grain reentrancy allows us to override turn-based concurrency and can process multiple messages on the same thread (Microsoft, n.d.). Since the grain is still limited to a single thread, it will alternate processing between the messages. This allows the grain to accept new work as the current process is waiting for an asynchronous procedure to complete. In other words, if we are calling the database asynchronously, another request can begin processing as we wait for the response.

Grain reentrancy does not come without risks from sharing a thread. The request may have a mutated state. That is, if a method execution has completed and another method is being continued, its state may not change. Also, implementing reentrant grains correctly can be complex.

Additional information can be found here: Reentrancy | Microsoft Orleans Documentation (dotnet.github.io).

External Tasks and Grains

Orleans uses a relatively small thread pool (determined by number of CPU cores in the system). Therefore, blocking a thread should be avoided as this will quickly reduce the thread pool's processing capabilities. If a blocked call is required – which should be rare – the grain can use the .NET thread pool (Microsoft, n.d.). Using *await* allows the blocking call to be made from the grain.

Grain Services

Grain Services runs from the startup task to the shutdown of every silo and does not have an identity. This is a long-running grain that can be used for ongoing processes. There are a few caveats, such as not writing to a stream directly, and we may not constantly be communicating with it on the originating silo.

Stateless Worker Grains

Stateless workers were created to support recurring work that is not tied to a single flow. For instance, if the same job, such as decrypting and encrypting messages, is needed for multiple workflows, the stateless worker can be used to accomplish the task. It is also scalable to handle growing requests. I like to think of these and common utilities like are sometimes build for microservice supporting services.

They run differently than ordinary grains:

- The messages will be sent to a newly activated grain rather than the queue of the existing grain. They are subject to the same garbage collection policy as ordinary grains.

- The stateless worker grain will always be activated on the same silo as the requesting grain.

- Additional workers are created automatically in case the current workers are busy.

- The default number of stateless worker activations on each silo is related to the number of CPU cores. This can be configured in the maxLocalWorker method when decorated as [`StatelessWorker(max LocalWorkers: 1)`].

- Individual stateless worker grains cannot be accessed, which means that multiple requests may be fulfilled by different instances of the stateless worker grain. Additional information can be found here: `https://dotnet.github.io/orleans/docs/grains/ stateless_worker_grains.html`

Grain Call Filters

Grain Call Filters allow us to intercept grain calls, enabling us to perform telemetry, authorization, event handling, and status updates by executing code before and after the grain work (Microsoft, n.d.). There are two kinds of incoming filters: receiving a call and outgoing, which is triggered when making a call.

Silos

Silo lifecycle:

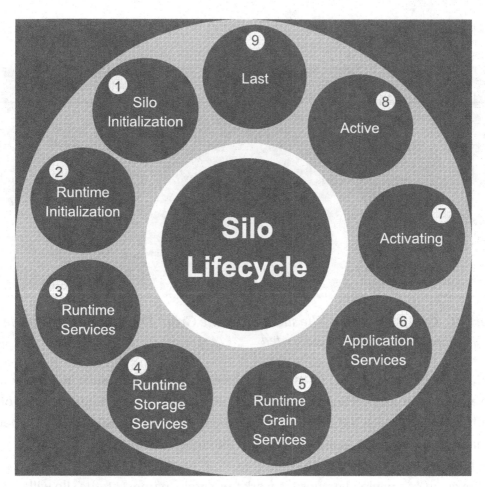

Figure 3-2. *Silo lifecycle. Each silo has its process of starting up, taking on work, and shutting down*

Silos are the runtimes for grains. A silo can maintain various kinds of grains and can join other silos to form a cluster. Silos also deactivate grains after a given idle time. Silos allow us to instantiate trillions of grains without having to write custom lifecycle coding. We do have to concern ourselves, in part, with cloud scaling thresholds, such as seen in Application Services in Azure. In order to determine thresholds, we would need to load test an individual instance and calculate min, max, and standard throughput based on historical or estimated traffic. The silo lifecycle, as shown in Figure 3-2, displays the steps of a silo starting, working, and shutting down. A graceful shutdown is initiated by disposing of the silo.

What makes this amazing is that the setup is trivial. The time saved, in comparison to frameworks such as Akka, is enormous. Orleans allows us to quickly jump into development. Otherwise, creating a silo is a large task to accomplish and would create a plethora of risks until it's been deemed stable and vetted.

Grain Directory

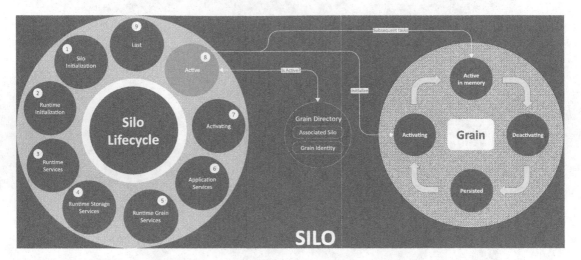

Figure 3-3. *Grain Directory. The silo queries the Grain Directory to determine if a grain is active or needed to be activated*

The Grain Directory is used to contains the current state of a grain, such as if it is active. Grains are continuously cycling between states, and payloads may require the use of a currently active grain. Each grain has a unique identifier, such as using a GUID, where grain-name-111 and grain-name-999 perform different work based on the intake, although they are of the same grain type.

In the event of a payload requesting work from grain-name-111, the silo will query the Grain Directory, as seen in Figure 3-3, to determine if the grain is active and determine the referenced server. If the grain is not active, the silo will create the grain and send the work to it. If the grain exists, then the work will be sent to the silo that owns it. A response will be returned to the sending silo if a reply is needed, which is then passed to the client.

The Grain Directory is part of Orleans' Server NuGet package (NuGet Gallery | Microsoft.Orleans.Server 3.5.1). It is an in-memory distributed hash table. Being new to Orleans, it is advised to use the default Grain Directory, although we can implement a Redis or Azure Storage version. Implement a pluggable version if there is a need:

- To minimize the number of grains that are deactivated when a silo is, within a cluster, shut down

- Of a stronger single-activation guarantee (Microsoft, n.d.)

As a best practice, it is advised to gain experience with Orleans before implementing a pluggable Grain Directory, but when you do attempt to start with the long-lived grains (Microsoft, n.d.).

Message Path

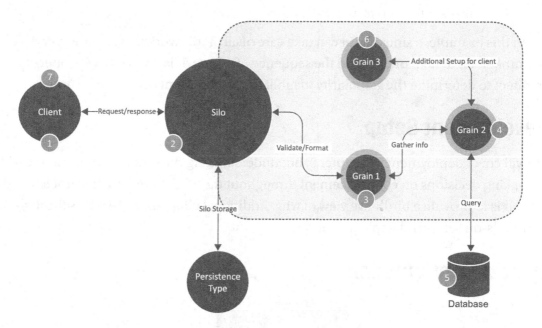

Figure 3-4. *Message flow. A request is passed from the client to the silo and then a message is given to the grain to begin work. When the work is completed and if a response is required, it will be passed back from the grain to the client through the silo.*

A request is passed through several items during its workflow. The silo is the runtime for the grains and passes messages between the grains and the client. Following the pathway shown in Figure 3-4

1. A client creates a request and sends it to the silo.

2. The silo gets the request and associates the grain call.

3. Grain 1 receives the message, and if the grain is busy, messages are queued, to observe the turn-based concurrency model, which executes the sub-tasks on the same thread. Grain 2 is sent a message to query information.

4. Grain 2 completes the information gathering and object mapping and then passes a message to Grain 3.

5. Grain 3 formats the message into the response format and passes the message back to Grain 2.

6. Grain 2 returns the information to Grain 1.

7. The response is returned to the client.

In this example, a single grain can take care of all of this work as well; however, this was broken up to help understand the sequence of events. It is up to the developer/architect to determine the granularity to fulfill the requirements of the application.

Development Setup

We will cover deployment in Chapter 9, but understanding the process is crucial. We will be making decisions on code placement throughout the book based on this process. This section is to provide a bird's-eye view of why. Additional chapters will walk us through the hands-on setup and implementation.

Typical Configuration

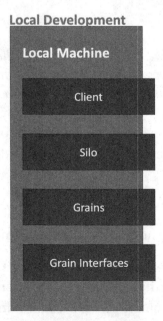

Figure 3-5. *Local development. Local development runs each project on the same machine*

In the example applications, we will dive further into the setup. It is important to know that the client, silo, grain(s), and grain interface(s) will exist in the same solution as seen in Figure 3-5. It will consist of two console applications, the client and the silo, and two .NET Core libraries, grains and grain interfaces. It is easier for us to develop projects in a single solution vs. separating projects into individual solutions, which is commonly used for DevSecOps. It is good practice to separate them for parallel or multi-team development; however, learning Orleans takes precedence at the moment, and the projects can be separated in the future.

Silo Configuration

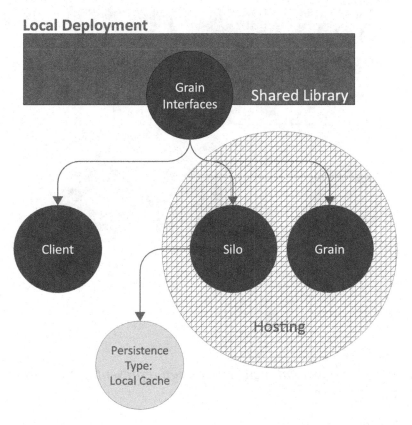

Figure 3-6. *Local deployment view. This is how the applications correspond on your local machine*

When we run Orleans in the local development setup, the client is a console application that sends requests to the silo. The libraries are shared through references in the application. Cluster persistence is set to use in-memory (volatile) storage, and it is set as a single silo. This client is a console application to simulate an actual client and pass requests. In a real-life scenario, the client would likely be an MVC application.

In Figure 3-6, we can see that all of the items live on the same machine. The silo is configured as a single silo, which means all of the grains will belong to it. The persisted objects will use the local machine's memory. The grain interfaces are shared between the projects by the bin directory and references. This setup allows a developer to run the application and send transactions through it quickly.

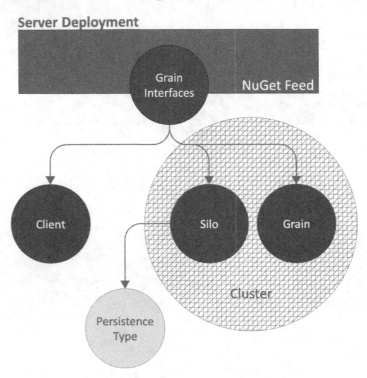

Figure 3-7. *Server deployment view. This design represents how entities correspond in a remote setup*

Production hosting is depicted differently to extend scalability and persistence. As shown in Figure 3-7, grain interfaces are shared via a NuGet feed. Feeds allow multiple applications to consume the same libraries without the applications being aware of each other. The persistence type can be extended to various hosting types of your choice and allows the flexibility of hosting on-premises and in multiple clouds.

- Silo persistence types:

- Azure Blob and Table Storages

- SQL Server

- Apache ZooKeeper

- Consul IO

- DynamoDB

- In-Memory

- Cosmo

Note   More persistence types are available on the OrleansContrib GitHub organization's site: `https://github.com/OrleansContrib/`.

Cluster

A cluster is a grouping of silos that are able to communicate with each other. The silos also monitor connectivity between one another. What this accomplishes is that if a silo fails and once the failure is detected, then the grains can be reinstantiated on another silo that supports the same type of grains. Assuming that there is another silo that supports the type of grains running, then clients will not be aware of the failure other than possible latency.

Silo Membership

Silo Membership allows silos to be aware of one another and join to form a cluster. This includes the ability where silos to determine the health of other silos and share it within the cluster. All executions are capable of being passed evenly across the silos (Microsoft, n.d.).

We can use this table for troubleshooting since it houses diagnostics. It is a centralized table that each silo, within the cluster, uses to determine the health of other silos. Basically, what happens is that the silos directly ping one another to determine if they are alive. You may be familiar with this technique when coding services for various cloud hosts, such as Pivotal, where a method is created in the service that returns a message to show that it is alive. The difference is that the silos ping one another and eventually create a virtual ring of the silos. This is called consistent hashing. This allows silos to be dropped from and added to the cluster, so the cluster as a whole is not disrupted.

Multi-clusters

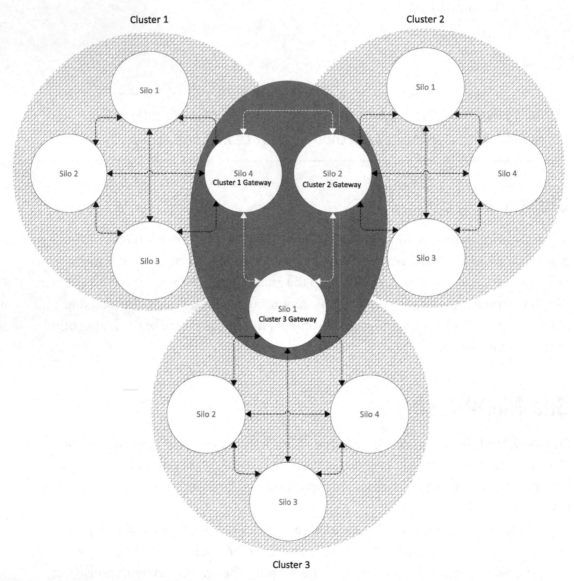

Figure 3-8. *Multi-cluster. Clusters are connected and use silos 4, 2, 1 as cluster gateways*

We can have clusters join other clusters and are able to pass messages between them, such as in Figure 3-8, where clusters 1, 2, and 3 are hosted in separate regions. Each cluster has its own identity, and Orleans automatically selects silos from each cluster to become cluster gateways. Cluster gateways advertise their IP addresses as a conduit for the cluster or initial contact. Instead of forcing all messages through cluster gateways, after the calling silo learns and caches where the grain is activated, it will communicate with that silo directly, even if it isn't a cluster gateway. Creating the ability to bypass cluster gateways helps prevent them from becoming bottlenecks.

Gossip Protocol

The Gossip Protocol is a process of peer-to-peer communication and is sometimes used in distributed systems. The way it works is that silos will randomly pair up and communicate information about other silos. This pairing will continue to occur, and the information will be shared among all of the silos within the cluster. This information is shared in the silo address that is used as the lookup key, which includes

- *Timestamp*

- *ClusterId*

- *Status* – Either Active or Inactive

In addition to Gossip, which identifies locations and statuses, the multi-cluster configuration shares if the cluster is

- Active or inactive

- Joined or non-joined

The multi-cluster can be injected into any cluster at any time and will then persist in the running silos and specified and persisted gossip channels. The single-instance protocol maintains mutual exclusion – in other words, shared resources cannot be accessed simultaneously – so that files, such as the configuration file, can be updated without issues.

The cluster configuration maintains the current status of the clusters. It allows the clusters in the multi-cluster to centralize the handling each other's statuses and reduce network congestion with unnessasary traffic. The communication would then be used from Gossip to communicate.

Additional information on the Gossip Protocol is found here: `www.sciencedirect.com/topics/computer-science/gossip-protocol`.

Journaled Grains

Journaled grains are able to receive notifications when a connection error is detected and also when it has been resolved (Microsoft, n.d.). This is done by overriding:

- OnConnectionIssue can report how long it has been since the last successful connection and additional information that helps determine the issue.

- OnConnectionIssueResoved will send a notification that the issue has been resolved by passing the same issue object that was used with OnConnectionIssue.

However, the sharing of data between the clusters does not synchronize immediately as there will be differences in the state as values are updated due to eventual consistency. Eventual consistency is defined as replicating the data across applications, on each application, perform updates tentatively locally, and propagate local updates to other applications asynchronously, when connections are available (Burckhardt, 2014).

Base statistics have also been added to the journaled grains; however, they are fairly new and will likely going to be expanded upon. At the moment they support

- EnableStateCollection to start the statistics gathering

- DisableStateCollection that stops the statistics gathering

- GetStats that retrieves the statistics for us to use

Additional information can be found here: `https://dotnet.github.io/orleans/docs/grains/event_sourcing/journaledgrain_diagnostics.html`.

Eventual Consistency

Eventual consistency is where a value, or in our case a state, will eventually share the latest updated state. If multiple nodes are storing the same "value" and that is updated in one of the nodes, the latest value will update the rest of the nodes for sharing. At some point, all of the nodes will share the latest value – in our case, the connectivity to a cluster or silo state. This means some silos will see the connection restored before others and eventually all of the silos will have the latest data.

Heterogeneous Silos

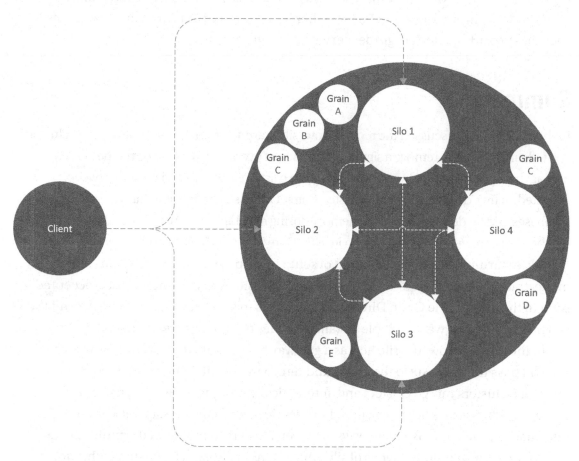

Figure 3-9. *Heterogeneous silos. Silos 1 and 2 are hosting grains A, B, and C. Silo 3 hosts grain E, and silo 4 hosts grains C and D (modified from Microsoft, Heterogeneous silos, n.d.)*

Heterogeneous silos consist of silos of different types, such as having access to GPUs while the others do not. As shown in Figure 3-9, we see that silos 1 and 2 both host grains A, B, and C, while silo 4 is hosting grains C and D, where D is unique to silo 4's type. Silo 3, which is a unique silo type, is the only silo that can host grain E. This mapping depicts that if silo 2 leaves the cluster, silo 1 will continue hosting grains A, B, and C and silo 4 hosting grain C. However, if silo 3 leaves the cluster, a runtime issue will occur since it is the only silo hosting grain E.

Having the ability to maintain several grain types creates redundancy if a silo fails. Unfortunately, they do not support stateless worker grain, which we covered above.

Additional information can be found here: `https://dotnet.github.io/orleans/docs/host/configuration_guide/server_configuration.html`.

Summary

In this chapter, we discussed the request flow, silo startup, grain life cycles and multi-clusters.

Orleans' lifecycles remove a significant burden of overhead from the developer. Grain management is supported by the silo. Each grain exists in memory and moves between activated, active, deactivated, and persisted states. Orleans can save states and data in extensive databases and be debugged in local memory during development. Also, due to the plethora of database allowances and being written in .NET Core/latest .NET, Orleans is cloud-agnostic.

Silo's startup has a decent amount of setup to prepare networking, grain orchestration, and ready-to-accept work. Once the silo is active, then work is accepted to send to the grains. The Grain Directory allows silos to know if the grain is active and the silo hosting it – that way, multiple instances of identical grains aren't created.

In the request flow, the silo acts as a gateway between the clients and the grains. The silo will pass the requests to the grains and return the result when completed.

Multi-clusters merge clusters and automatically designate silos as cluster gateways; however, all messages are not required to pass through them. Gossip network shares information, such as cluster gateways, between clusters to maintain the multi-cluster.

There are also different types of silos that grains are able to be hosted with, such as with GPUs. The silos can support the types of grains as needed; however, if the only remaining type of a silo that is able to support the grain is removed from the cluster, for any reason, the calls will result in a runtime error.

We have also covered a high-level view of local and production configuration. When starting a project, it is set up for local development.

Also, we learned that there are items that live outside the lifecycles, such as stateless workers which as used as common utility services in a microservice pattern. A personal word of caution when creating utility services/grains is to name them appropriately otherwise they have the ability to bloat. For example, a service utility is generic and can continue to house items where if the utility is an Image Conversion Service, then the name forms the scope of the supported features.

Clusters are capable of being heterogeneous to support multiple types of grains. Clusters can connect to other clusters and become multi-clusters. Multi-clusters use journaled grains since they can report connectivity issues. It may take some time for all of the silos to become aware of the state of the connectivity due to eventual consistency.

The next chapter will review monolithic, stateless three-tier microservices, and Orleans architectures and attributes. It will help us understand when to write specific architectures that should be used based on the business needs. The designs and frameworks can be leveraged in various use cases.

## CHAPTER 4

Enhancing Current Designs

Overview

We are determining which tool matches the requirements of the given application. A monolithic application may not always need to be broken down for future growth since the value isn't worth the cost.

We will discuss the pros and cons between monolithic and microservice applications and Orleans and how Orleans can enhance monolithic and microservice development.

Monolithic applications, in many cases, are easier to debug and trace since a developer can follow a single payload through the application. A monolithic application can be a great tool when there isn't a need for separated services for individual scalability for functions that may be bottlenecks. Also, Kubernetes is able to sustain large applications, which can remove the need to create a microservice solution, which reduces a lot of design overhead. Monoliths were used for decades and can still be a strong choice due to ease of setup and basic deployment needs.

With any solution there are negative connotations as well. Monolithic applications live in the gray area where there aren't defined scopes and the application can grow immensely. There have been cases where legacy applications have grown to the point where they are supported by several teams. Since the application is tightly coupled, the synchronization between team project completions and external application dependencies severely hinder deployment. There are fewer pipelines to deploy; however, the seemingly simplified deployment shifts away from technical solutions and toward project management growth where teams must complete projects before due dates. Granted, the added feature could be turned on through multiple updates with the use of feature flags.

© Thomas Nelson 2022
T. Nelson, *Introducing Microsoft Orleans*, https://doi.org/10.1007/978-1-4842-8014-0_4

Microservices allow development teams to scale while increasing flexibility by being able to be written in multiple languages, scalability due to application-scoped sizes, and reduced overall development effort, per service, thanks to loosely coupled services. The defined scope allows teams to know where features should be placed as well as the team ownership. The scope reduces the growth and keeps the service fairly core to its needs. In summary, microservice applications are constructed in three tiers that consist of the client interface, business logic, and the database layers. Each is a separated, decoupled component with a much smaller scope. This book's context will focus on the three-tier model, which is common and simplifies the comparison between the frameworks and architectures. The architecture is a newer design priming applications for cloud-native solutions.

However, these solutions do not come without overhead, such as determining how to design and implement the services to work in a holistic manner. Each service will also need a place to be hosted and pipelines to deploy them to the environments. These require more deployment setup effort, in terms of deployment pipelines, and individual attention to max and average load to determine the scaling required per service. Scaling is referred to as scaling up (aka vertical), which adds additional hardware resources to the virtual machines such as RAM and processors, or scaling out (aka horizontal), which creates another instance of the application. Endpoints can be versioned as features are extended along with implementing an additional tool that connects services and API Management, which adds security and rate limiting.

Orleans requires interfaces to be implemented when adding grains. This forces a loosely coupled design and scopes the grains. It combines attributes from the database, such as transactions, and incorporates them in the application tier. This unlocks high scalability as you can use basic data stores with a low set of guarantees and still maintain consistency and concurrency. Orleans also orchestrates the scaling of the grains as needed, without the support and monitoring of the platform.

The framework can be seen as a monolithic service or support the back end of microservices or legacy applications. Essentially, Orleans can be seen as a megalith application that can house a massive amount of smaller services; however, the size is not enforced. The services, grains, will require less effort than the microservices since they don't require developers to set up endpoint routing, scale thresholds, or establish network connections between grains. Orleans removes the need for developers to have to understand a substantial amount related to how an actor model framework orchestrates and communicate within the cluster.

Unfortunately, the actor model is not usually covered in schools, which leaves a gap in understanding in the technology sector. Orleans design setup is a bit different if you are coming from a traditional monolithic or microservice architecture. This is not something to be concerned about since the framework was built to be easily understood and we will walk you through the setup.

Monolithic services and microservices are viable options for development. Orleans can enhance their ability to scale and separation of duties and automatically orchestrate the backend code. We will see how the various patterns differ and how Orleans can remove barriers, save money, and simplify future developments and deployments.

General Comparison

Legacy applications can start as any size, and with any application, features are added to extend the service overtime. Since these applications are not scoped, many features can be appended overtime, which allow them to grow into monolithic applications. These are not necessarily bad since we can usually walk through the entire application. This allows developers to understand the application and debug it. Unfortunately, it can become difficult to deploy when several teams are working on dependencies, which can lead to a cascading delay in deployment. What I mean by this is if components required are being developed by separate teams and each needs to be developed in a sequential manner due to hierarchical logic, then any delay in an upstream team will impact the downstream team. In contrast, microservices can be developed in parallel based on an alignment of the payload(s) being passed. The monolithic application may incur tech debt if it does require a waterfall approach since that can add risk to a deployment deadline.

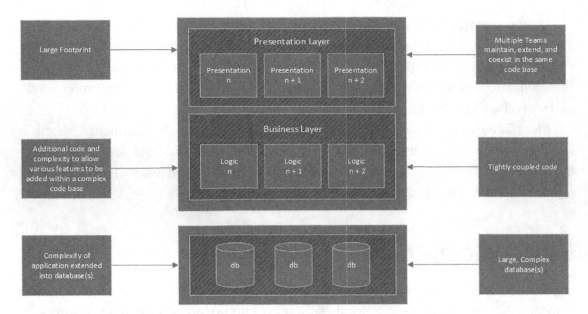

Figure 4-1. *Monolithic application example. The figure displays an example of a structure of a monolithic application. Each application could grow to support multiple presentation layers and various scopes in the business layer. Due to not having a scope, features can continuously be added to the application to support more logic and interfaces from current and future external applications as well*

A legacy application is extensive where multiple team workflows may exist in the same application, shown in Figure 4-1. The presentation and business layers deploy as a single entity, which makes deployments relatively easy. If testing is implemented from the creation of the monolith, it will reduce a large amount of risk, although it can be a daunting work for an aged application, just from sheer size, that has zero to little unit tests and functional tests implemented. In short, if we implement good common practices, such as SOLID, in a monolith, the risk of issue is significantly reduced.

From a DevOps perspective, a single deployment pipeline does not always mean that all items are ready to be deployed. As an added risk, if there are multiple teams supporting a single application and the release fails, specifically in production, it may be difficult to determine who owns the failure and how to fix it. It may be a failure that involves multiple teams, which adds complexity and possibly more time to determine a correction.

It is important to understand that a monolithic application will have a larger footprint than microservices, which can affect the time to scale out in comparison to a single microservice. What I mean by this is the amount of resources and the complexity of the application need to be taken into account when the scaling threshold is triggered.

The timing from being triggered to when the new instance is ready to start receiving work will likely be larger than microservices. The monolith does have greater availability overall since it is a single service that is running rather than multiple services that can be seen as multiple points of failure running as a holistic approach.

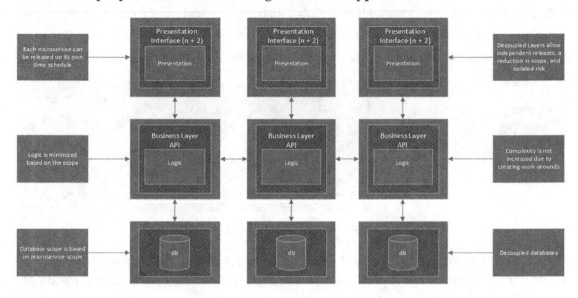

Figure 4-2. *Microservice application. Each service is smaller when compared with the legacy applications due to defined scopes. APIs can pass messages to one another and traditionally have dedicated databases, which are confined to the needs of the microservices*

As seen in Figure 4-2, the separation of the applications allows developers to determine where features should be added or used by other services. For instance, a book service would be used to look up and determine the quantity of books. Other services can call on this service, and if it generates more traffic, multiple instances can be stood up to support the traffic. This is what differentiates microservices from monolithic applications in that specific services of what would be the entire monolith can be scaled as needed.

Scopes are generally handled by the naming of the application and proper oversight by architects and lead/senior developers. The scope keeps the code specific to its determined need and reduces redundant code since other services would call this service rather than adding it to their service. Over my time as a developer, I have seen multiple code redundancies in several legacy applications due to teams not documenting items and adding quick fixes. Microservices help reduce this issue without having to know the entire code base.

Cloud hosting supports the ability to scale based on items such as CPU usage. Cloud architecture, the size, and the independence of microservices allow this to be easily handled and quickly. Duplicating instances across regions is more affordable while also reducing the overhead, primarily when the cloud maintains scalability. Smaller, decoupled services work very well on a global distribution scale since different portions of a system might be more popular with different customers based on locations. Books might require more instances in one region of the globe, while movies are in another.

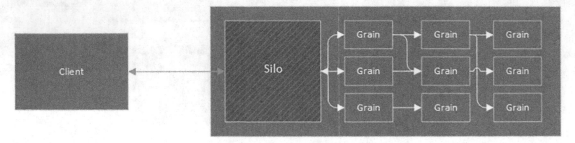

Note: Multiple silos in cluster

Figure 4-3. *Orleans framework. A client will send a message to the silo, which sends the message to a grain to complete the process and possibly return a message to the client*

The Orleans architecture may seem a bit different in comparison to the other designs you are likely more accustomed to but can be used as a back end for either. Logic is broken down to smaller classes by forcing IoC --although there is not a grain size restraint, IoC generally forces smaller coding sections--, which allows a smaller footprint and grants the ability to scale out significantly faster than microservices and always accept work. Resource usage is specific to the request rather than requiring resources to run another microservice or monolithic application to take specific requests. For instance, imagine a grain handles a shopping cart, while a monolith encompasses the entire website of searching for items, cart, and checkout or a microservice handles shopping, which includes the cart and other functions. If the shopping is needed to be scaled in each of these items, the monolith would have to create a new instance of the entire application, and the microservice would have to do the same with the shopping cart. Orleans would only create additional instances of the cart. Additionally, the grains will wait for a managed period of time before being persisted and deactivated incase additional work is requested.

Also, the silo manages the scaling (creation of initial grains required since each grain is unique) of the grains, displayed in Figure 4-3, rather than relying on the cloud platform. Each grain is decoupled inherently through the framework requiring interfaces. The silo is independent, as is the client.

As mentioned before, the client can also be a proxy. The client calls the silo by using the interfaces. If you would like to allow clients to communicate with Orleans without worrying about sharing libraries, then a proxy client will fill this need. The proxy can house the interfaces and interface with the silo while sharing endpoints (API Management, Swagger, Public, Internal).

Orleans' framework can be used in both monolith and microservice designs or seen as either. Orleans is a framework, and we show how it works under the covers and can be interwoven into either design type. We can think of Orleans as a monolith containing decoupled projects services. These abilities can be used to extend the monolithic application or microservice's back end. The scaling is handled by the framework rather than the platform.

Elasticity and Availability Comparisons

Elasticity is the ability of the application to meet the on-demand needs of the workload. The quicker an application can scale out/in, the higher its elasticity. Elasticity is used to mitigate the risk of delaying or failing to support the unscheduled burst of requests. The ability to quickly and efficiently scale also helps reduce resources being consumed.

For instance, an application that is capable of handling 100 transactions is suddenly receiving 300 requests simultaneously. The trigger (CPU usage, transactions, messages in the queue, etc.) will start the event to create additional instances of the application to handle the workload. Once the work has been completed, the other instances can be deactivated, and resources are returned to the server.

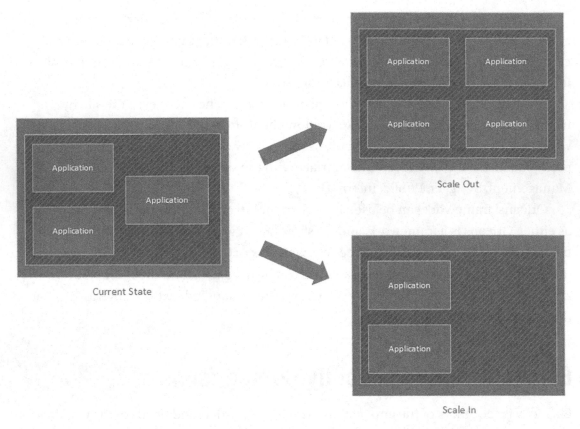

Figure 4-4. *Scaling. The figure displays instance states to support the current state of incoming requests. Elasticity can scale both inward and outward*

Based on the example of 100 requests growing to 300, additional instances will be created to handle the unforeseen workload. As we can see in Figure 4-4, instances are created to support the new need and deactivated based on workload. The issue that depicts the difference between legacy, microservice, and virtual actor applications is the speed and monitoring to be elastic.

Let us reevaluate the example based on each application type:

- Legacy application

  - It may take longer for the new instance to accept work based on the size and complexity of the application startup time.

  - Monitoring and scaling is dependent on the platform.

- Microservice

- Microservice instances will typically take less time to scale than monolithic instances due to the smaller footprint.

- Monitoring and scaling is dependent on the platform.

- Grain

  - Nearly instantaneously.

  - Monitoring and scaling is dependent on the framework, which allows a faster response to workloads.

  - Orleans can activate grains without the monitoring of a platform, and it can scale for size with the platform as needed.

It is essential to pay attention to the time frame while waiting for the instances to start receiving traffic, when setting up a new application. Two common ways that risk is reduced are by adding a queue and setting the threshold that triggers the scaling low enough to provide padded time while the instances are activating. Both solutions add complexity and need to be compared:

- Adding a queue requires the ability to pop messages from the queue. Multiple tools can accomplish this task, such as an event-driven or a queue listener.

- We can set the threshold trigger lower, which allows the instance to stand up earlier. Resource consumption will likely be higher and affect the overall cost.

The quicker an instance can be ready for work, the fewer workarounds are required. Risk is reduced by not attempting to solve an issue based on an educated guess of a threshold setting and assumed timing. Otherwise, adding a queue causes additional possible failure points and costs.

Since grains can receive work at any time, a workaround is not required. A silo can receive the request and immediately create a grain. If additional requests require the exact grain and it hasn't been decommissioned, it is still in memory. The framework allows the silo to maintain elasticity rather than making changes to the architecture or relying on a slower cloud monitoring threshold tool. The size, simplicity, asynchronicity, and running in memory allow it to happen virtually in real time.

Availability allows services to continue to receive and process work during maintenance. Every application will need to be updated at some point, whether it is for security, additional features, or newly found bugs. It was common for websites to go offline and a maintenance page to alert users of downtime. This was accomplished, and still is in some cases, by deploying updates during low traffic time, which usually occurs late weekend nights and requires the staff to deploy and test and possibly correct and redeploy. The longer the site is down directly impacts the company's ability to do business and may deter future users whom may see it as an unstable website. The money loss places pressure on the team(s) to complete the deployment quickly and without incident.

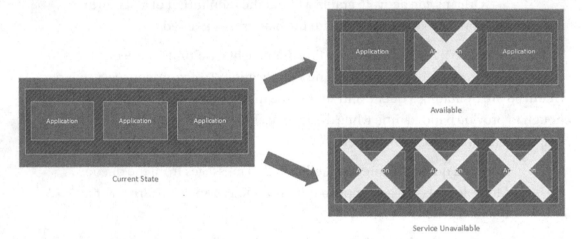

Figure 4-5. *Maintenance periods. Services are available during maintenance periods. The figure displays a service available in the upper section vs. not being reached in the lower area*

Cloud architecture allows services to be taken offline while they are being updated. Additional PaaS services such as Kubernetes allow rolling updates – wait for the activity to be completed before updating to a newer version where the subsequent transactions are worked – and app services use slots that can deploy in an A/B pattern that allows a percentage of traffic to be routed to the updated application. In Figure 4-5, we can see the server/application taken offline while two others continue to accept traffic.

The cloud tools that support these options perform them wonderfully; however, there is an associated cost. Azure's App Service requires a higher tier to scale automatically. Orleans supports rolling updates. It handles the update in a different fashion. The new silo is added to the cluster, and the old silo is able to access the new and old grains, while the new silo can only access the new grains. Validations can be done, and if everything is deemed successful, there's a silo swap, and the original will migrate to the newer silo activations. Otherwise, the newer silo version can be shut down, and the initial grain instances will be created.

There are pros and cons to these aspects. Cloud platforms allow monolithic/ microservice applications to be updated in an easy manner, such as by using Azure Deployment slots where a new deployment can take none to all of the public traffic, which allows things like smoke testing.

However, this does not mean that deploying on-premises in this manner is easy. It requires infrastructure setup that sets load balancing, deployments to specific machines, and rollback abilities. Orleans updates can be handled in the same manner of deploying an updated silo on-prem or in the cloud. The downside is that it is extra work for DevOps engineers for an initial setup, especially compared to containers being deployed to slots. This means there will be different-looking pipelines to maintain, although the Orleans pipeline will not change as drastically when deploying between on-prem vs. in the cloud.

Business Logic Complexity

Business logic complexity is always an issue when it comes to maintaining a product. As discussed, microservices split sections of logic into the specific scope that decouples logic for easier maintainability and individual scaling, and the separation allows individual services to be updated independently. Monolith applications can create the need to complete several sections of code before being able to deploy, which can delay time frames. Grains can be long-running and complex; however, they are required to run on a single thread.

Orleans logic is handled much like microservices in that each grain can be written and updated on its own and it is decoupled. This allows modular updates and matches the common microservice approach. This tactic also allows Orleans to alleviate the need to introduce and maintain feature flags, particularly in the monolithic application code. Again, monolithic applications are being referred to as the all-in-one application without scope boundaries. Orleans is the framework that can extend either of these design patterns.

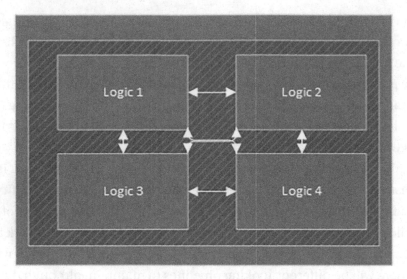

Figure 4-6. *Monolithic application logic mapping. Logic can call out to any library at any time within this application. It makes it extremely difficult to know how to keep track of what has been completed, the flow, and how to implement changes*

Without decoupling logic, it can be hard to determine what has been written and where to find different sections of logic. We should also construct the logic with the foresight of easier maintenance and deployments. As we can see in Figure 4-6, any library can talk to the other. Multilevel communication points are not the case by default; however, personnel change/leave positions, and hardened rules deteriorate overtime. As new items are required and the application is nearly a decade-old, then management changes and possibly reorganizations have happened within that time frame. Deadlines and the lack of understanding of the application's initial requirements and its architecture lead to items being added to "just work."

Let's now state that a different team owns each logic(n). Each team will need to stay in sync on delivery and current development states. Not staying in constant sync can lead to a domino effect across the groups. Any delay will force the teams to miss release dates and live through far too many status meetings.

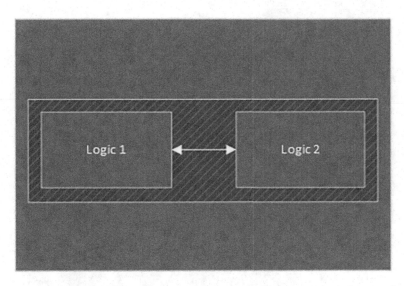

Figure 4-7. *Microservice logic mapping. The applications are decoupled and communicate through REST endpoints. Endpoints can be version controlled so that the requestor can update on their schedule*

Logic is focused and generally transferred through REST endpoints. Endpoints allow APIs to use a globally standardized transaction protocol of HTTP(s), shown in Figure 4-7. The applications also remain small as long as the team is educated in microservices and stays diligent. In my experience, the naming of the microservice is vital, as it defines the scope. A microservice named Utility can quickly grow into a bloated monolithic application. In comparison, a service called BillingValidation or Billing – depending on the size of the company/work – creates a logical understanding of the scope.

Complex business logic can be easily maintained and updated. Let us assume a separate team owns each service. Each team can update and deploy without having to sync deployment schedules. The deployment type is dependent on the resources that host it, such as virtual machines, app engines/services, Kubernetes, etc.

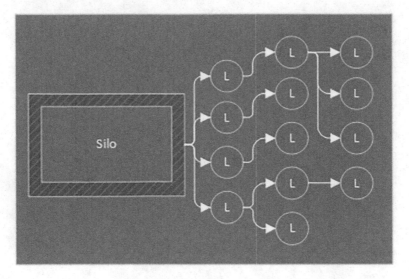

Figure 4-8. *Orleans logic mapping. Logic can run on a single thread. Each grain can create another grain to perform additional actions*

Grains can house simple logic and call out other grains to perform additional actions, accomplishing reasonably complex tasks. Figure 4-8 shows how various paths are available depending on the transaction's needs – adhering to the fundamental pillars of single-threaded scoped logic built into the framework that forces a team to comply with the scope.

Attempting to maintain pathways of the grains can be a challenging feat though. Naming conventions, such as we discussed concerning microservices, can apply here. Unlike the monolithic services and microservices, the resource does not dictate the deployment. Orleans can deploy rolling updates through the framework.

In a way, we can see the Orleans framework take aspects of each design and reduce the complexity of the overall design that you choose to use. Orleans maintains scoped development that we can find with microservice principles. It includes the ability of cross-team-single-solution approach that is commonly found in monolithic development practices that can be deployed with a single pipeline.Also, multi-clusters, which were covered in Chapter 3, provide an easily regional or globally scaling solution. The enforced IoC generally breaks the logic into smaller classes that are decoupled and scoped. In either case, Orleans has aspects of development that we have used in the past, which significantly reduces the learning curve.

Deployment

Accomplishing deployment requires dependencies discovered and aligned. Depending on the software model, dependencies are challenging to find and correspond to deployment times. As the software grows and the company matures, what are some of the issues that may occur before deployment?

Dependency discovery

- Determine what applications are affected by the changes. Decoupled designs such as microservices severely reduce this effort. I have spent weeks in meetings with teams involved in tightly coupled applications before determining an aligned release date.

    - The Orleans framework brings this ability to the monolithic back ends.

Dependency alignment

- Teams that are affected by the changes have to deploy at the same time to continue working correctly. Architects will share contracts, and management allocates resources to complete the objectives. It can be difficult to determine which teams are affected in monolithic applications, which can result in teams not being aware until it is last in the development process.

- Microservices are easy to maintain with clear-cut sections of ownership, decoupling, and version control.

    - Teams do not need to be contacted for every deployment since Orleans naturally supports rolling updates. Monolithic services and microservices can also use rolling updates with Kubernetes; however, it is not *part* of the application.

- Orleans allows teams to identify grains in the same manner microservices are and makes determining dependencies much easier in monolith designs.

Functional tests

- Functional testing passes payloads into the application and verifies the results. These are different from unit tests, as unit tests focus on a small code section, whereas functional tests mock clients. These tests do take longer than unit tests since they do run various routes in the application.

- Monolithic applications can take a significant amount of time to test all due to excessive pathway testing.

- Microservices and Orleans perform these actions much faster since the scope of the application is defined.

Load tests

- Load tests bombard the application until it is deemed unsteady. These are also used to determine the default amount of instances based on expected traffic.

- The tests will allow the discovery of time frames for instances to scale out and help create an educated guess of the trigger threshold.

- Orleans handles grain activation automatically.

As we can see, deployment combines a significant amount of team effort. Dependencies, including the hosting technology, impact the ease of deployment. It can be hard to determine dependencies in intertwined, complex code. The Orleans framework enforces the size and complexity of the logic and interfaces for decoupling. Also, deployment is handled through the framework and not dependent on the hosting technology. Orleans does a beautiful job at enforcing decoupling, which reduces software and team dependency while also not depending on hosting technology to determine deployment paths. Using Orleans as a monolith or microservice back end can bring these attributes to your project.

Summary

In this chapter, we discussed the different types of service structures and how they compare. Monolithic services are extensive, all-encompassing applications that are generally maintained and extended by multiple teams. Microservices were developed from monolithic applications and need to be decoupled, scoped, and maintainable for development team scalability. Orleans took it a step further with many tiny services designed for cloud architecture that are scoped, decoupled, and maintainable while including hyper-scalability and concurrency. The framework allows these attributes to be added to your monolithic or microservice back end.

We covered several service topics and compared each service – monolithic, traditional three-tier, and Orleans – type's abilities:

- Scaling out

  - Monolithic and three-tier services are dependent on the hosting environment by being monitored and orchestrated.

  - Orleans' grains are activated and orchestrated by the silo and can work in conjunction with cloud hosting scaling such as Kubernetes.

  - The service's size/complexity is a factor in determining the scaling threshold to compensate for the time frame of allocating resources to when the new service can begin accepting work.

- Maintenance periods (minimize downtime)

  - Monolithic and three-tier services are dependent on the environment and if it allows A/B and rolling updates.

  - Orleans can be updated with rolling updates.

- Business logic

  - Monolithic services are generally hard to maintain since work is not scoped and several teams generally have to work together to add features.

  - Microservices are decoupled, and a single team maintains individual services. Versioning REST endpoints also reduce the need to synchronize with other teams when adding features.

  - The Orleans framework forces the developer to implement interfaces and small classes and shares this ability with microservice and monolithic designs.

- Transaction time

  - Monolithic services and microservices are likely to inherit latency when adding queues and waiting for services to scale out.

  - Orleans' grains are built with queues and can accept work at any time.

- Deployment

  - Monolithic applications have many dependencies that will likely need to be orchestrated between teams before deployment. It can be difficult to determine dependencies and ownership of items. Also, testing can take additional time, when compared to microservices, due to the breadth of logic and the amount of tests that have to be run to cover the application.

  - Microservices and Orleans have clearly scoped services, logic, and team ownership. Testing should not take an extensive amount of time because the logic is minimized per service.

  - Orleans can be used in both microservice and monolith designs.

In the next chapter, we will get some hands-on experience where we set up our project. We will cover the creation of the silo, client, grain, and grain interface. The application will also display how grains are activated.

## CHAPTER 5

Starting Development

Overview

Since we have covered the background of Orleans and how it can be helpful in your projects, let's dive into creating our first application. Now we can start getting some hands-on experience.

In this chapter, we will walk through the process of setting up our first Orleans project. First, we will step through the process of setting up the solution and adding each project. Then we will populate and run the solution to see Orleans in action.

Composition

Let's look at what we are building. First, we construct an application in the typical local development layout discussed earlier by adding all of the projects to a single solution.

© Thomas Nelson 2022
T. Nelson, *Introducing Microsoft Orleans*, https://doi.org/10.1007/978-1-4842-8014-0_5

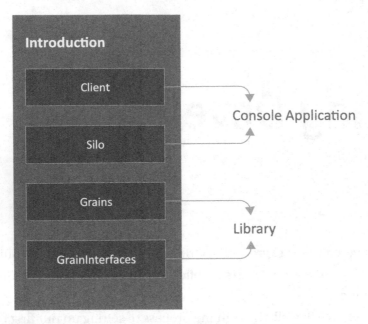

Figure 5-1. *Solution composition. The solution consists of four projects. Two of the projects, Client and Silo, are console applications. The other two, Grains and GrainInterfaces, are libraries*

As we can see in Figure 5-1, the solution will house four projects. We will walk through adding the two console applications and two libraries. Then we will implement our NuGet packages.

Building Our First Application

First, we create a new solution and a library project as a starting point using Visual Studio, or the CLI. Using Visual Studio, you can choose the Blank Solution template or choose to create the library project, which will also create the solution containing the library project, using .NET 5.0. From there, we will add two additional console projects and another library.

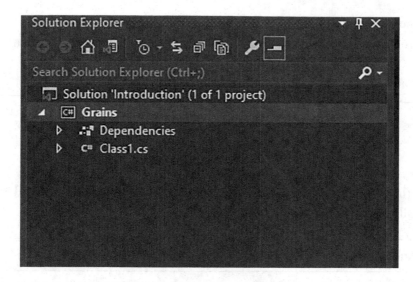

Figure 5-2. *Initial solution. The solution and first project are created*

Let us start by creating a new solution named "Introduction" and a .NET Core library called "Grains." The solution should resemble Figure 5-2.

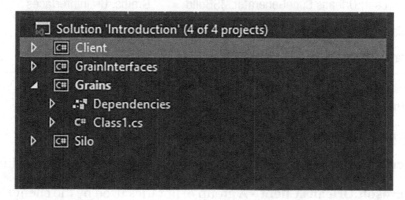

Figure 5-3. *Projects in a solution. The solution is comprised of Client, GrainInterfaces, Grains, and Silo*

Then add the additional projects of Silo, Client, and GrainInterfaces as shown in Figure 5-3. Silo and Client are both console applications, and GrainInterfaces is another .NET Core library like the Grains project. Finally, we should delete the default classes, Class1.cs, that were created with Grains and GrainInterfaces.

References:

Make sure you add the project references so the projects can communicate.

Project(s)	Reference
Grains, Silo, Client	GrainInterfaces
Silo	Grains

Afterward, we need to add the NuGet packages into each project. We will add the projects as follows:

NuGet Package	Add to Project(s)
Microsoft.Extensions.Logging.Console	Silo, Client
Microsoft.Orleans.Server	Silo
Microsoft.Orleans.Client	Client
Microsoft.Orleans.CodeGenerator.MSBuild	Grains, GrainInterfaces
Microsoft.Orleans.Core.Abstractions	Grains, GrainInterfaces
Microsoft.Extensions.Logging.Abstractions	Grains

Definitions:

- **Microsoft.Extensions.Logging.Console** – Logs to the console

- **Microsoft.Orleans.Server** – A collection of libraries used for hosting

- **Microsoft.Orleans.Client** – A group of libraries used by the client to communicate with Orleans

- **Microsoft.Orleans.CodeGenerator.MSBuild** – Uses Roslyn to generate code at runtime, uses .NET reflection for analysis

- **Microsoft.Orleans.Core.Abstractions** – Includes many items such as interfaces, errors, and base grain items

- **Microsoft.Extensions.Logging.Abstractions** – Includes the ability to log and the logging levels

To view a list of additional Orleans NuGet packages, visit `https://dotnet.github.io/orleans/docs/resources/nuget_packages.html`.

Currently, our solution should resemble Figure 5-4.

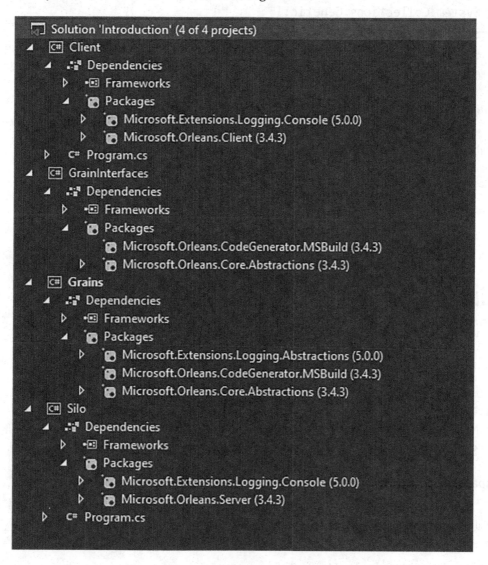

Figure 5-4. *Solution with NuGet packages*

Now we will begin adding the classes and base setup to the projects. Microsoft was kind enough to publish the templates for us to get started with.

Grain Interface

```
using System;
using System.Collections.Generic;
using System.Text;
using System.Threading.Tasks;
using Orleans;

namespace Introduction
{
    public interface ITutorial : Orleans.IGrainWithStringKey
    {
        Task<string> RespondWithCurrentTime(string message);
    }
}
```

Grain

This is where the work is being done. The grain received the message through the "RespondWIthCurrentTime" method and appended "was received at <current datetime>".

```
using System;
using Microsoft.Extensions.Logging;
using System.Threading.Tasks;

namespace Introduction
{
    public class TutorialGrain : Orleans.Grain, ITutorial
    {
        private readonly ILogger logger;

        //logger instance is set through the constructor
        public TutorialGrain(ILogger<TutorialGrain> logger)
        {
            this.logger = logger;
        }
```

```
public Task<string> RespondWithCurrentTime(string message)
{
    logger.LogInformation($"\n  message received: '{message}'");
    return Task.FromResult($"\n '{message}' was received at
    {DateTime.Now}");
}
}
}
```

*Note: We are passing all messages asynchronously.

Silo

First, let's start with setting up the server. The code for the silo and part of the client can be found at https://dotnet.github.io/orleans/docs/tutorials_and_samples/ tutorial_1.html and in our repo. The tutorial on the website creates a hello world; however, we will be expanding beyond as we continue. We start by placing the code in the Silo Program.cs file.

```
using System;
using System.Threading.Tasks;
using Microsoft.Extensions.Logging;
using Orleans;
using Orleans.Configuration;
using Orleans.Hosting;

namespace Introduction
{
    public class Program
    {
        public static int Main(string[] args)
        {
            return RunMainAsync().Result;
        }

        private static async Task<int> RunMainAsync()
        {
```

```
        try
        {
            var host = await StartSilo();
            Console.WriteLine("\n\n Press Enter to terminate...\n\n");
            Console.ReadLine();

            await host.StopAsync();

            return 0;
        }
        catch (Exception ex)
        {
            Console.WriteLine(ex);
            return 1;
        }
    }

    private static async Task<ISiloHost> StartSilo()
    {
        // define the cluster configuration
        var builder = new SiloHostBuilder()
            .UseLocalhostClustering()
            .Configure<ClusterOptions>(options =>
            {
                options.ClusterId = "dev";
                options.ServiceId = "Introduction";
            })
            .ConfigureApplicationParts(parts => parts.AddApplication
            Part(typeof(TutorialGrain).Assembly).WithReferences())
            .ConfigureLogging(logging => logging.AddConsole());

        var host = builder.Build();
        await host.StartAsync();
        return host;
    }
}
}
```

A couple items are needed to be known about the silo code:

- **UseLocalhostClustering()** is the method that sets Orleans to run on the local machine.

- **ConfigureApplicationParts** is responsible for referencing the application parts associated with the silo (Microsoft, n.d.).

- **ClusterId** is used to determine the grouping and will be required for multi-clusters.

  - **GossipChannels** is needed for multi-clusters for communication between clusters.

- **ServiceId** is an identifier for this service. Services with unique ids can use the same gossip channel.

Client

Update the "Project.cs" class by adding the following code to communicate with Orleans. In this example, we are calling the GrainId by a string name. A timestamp with the GrainId will be sent to the grain, and the response will include the original message and the timestamp from the grain. If the grain has not been created, it will be through the runtime; otherwise, the previously created grain will be activated or respond from an already active state – based on time and where it fits in the grain lifecycle – and that is where we will get our response.

```
using Microsoft.Extensions.Logging;
using Orleans;
using Orleans.Configuration;
using System;
using System.Threading.Tasks;
```

```
namespace Introduction
{
    public class Program
    {
        static int Main(string[] args)
        {
            return RunMainAsync().Result;
        }

        private static async Task<int> RunMainAsync()
        {
            try
            {
                using (var client = await ConnectClient())
                {
                    //Calling the method for use to interface with grains
                    await DoClientWork(client);
                    Console.ReadKey();
                }

                return 0;
            }
            catch (Exception e)
            {
                Console.WriteLine($"\nException while trying to run client:
                {e.Message}");
                Console.WriteLine("Make sure the silo the client is trying
                to connect to is running.");
                Console.WriteLine("\nPress any key to exit.");
                Console.ReadKey();
                return 1;
            }
        }
```

```csharp
private static async Task<IClusterClient> ConnectClient()
{
    IClusterClient client;
    client = new ClientBuilder()
        .UseLocalhostClustering()
        .Configure<ClusterOptions>(options =>
        {
            options.ClusterId = "dev";
            options.ServiceId = "Introduction";
        })
        .ConfigureLogging(logging => logging.AddConsole())
        .Build();

    await client.Connect();
    Console.WriteLine("Client successfully connected to silo
    host \n");
    return client;
}

private static async Task DoClientWork(IClusterClient client)
{
    bool repeat = true;

    do
    {
        // Grain Identity
        Console.WriteLine("What is the grain id?");
        string grainId = Console.ReadLine();

        // Call Specific Grain
        var example = client.GetGrain<ITutorial>(grainId);

        //Send Message with time stamp
        var response = await example.RespondWithCurrentTime($" This
        is {grainId} at {DateTime.Now}");
```

```
            //View response
            Console.WriteLine($"\n\n{response}\n\n");

            //Continue the example
            Console.WriteLine("Continue? Y/N");
            string continueResponse = Console.ReadLine();

            if (continueResponse.ToUpper() == "N")
            {
                repeat = false;
            }

        } while (repeat);

        return;
    }
  }
}
```

During the creation of this application, the highest stable libraries were used. Also, .NET 6 is still in preview, so we are using .NET Core 3.1. .NET 6 will be supported in the future as there are preview packages; however, I would prefer to work in stable libraries while learning the framework. You are welcome to explore the newer libraries on your own.

Our solution should look like the following version:

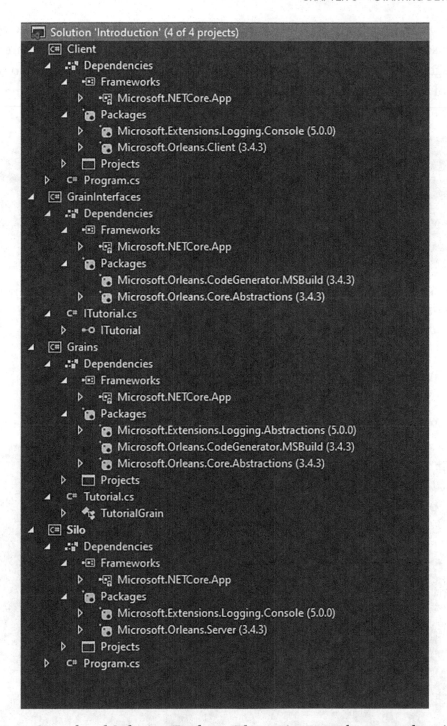

Figure 5-5. *Completed Solution Explorer. The projects, packages, and project references have been included*

After completing the setup, make sure to validate that the packages, not the versions, match those seen in Figure 5-5. Also, let's compile the solution (F6) to make sure all of the packages have been downloaded. After validating the items, we will need to run an instance of the silo and then the client. The silo needs to be ready before starting the client; otherwise, the client will time out.

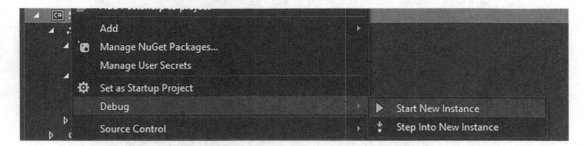

Figure 5-6. *Project instance creation. Start an instance of an individual project. To get to this menu, right-click the project and then mouse over "Debug" to display "Start New Instance"*

1. We need to start the silo and wait until it has completed its startup process, as shown in Figure 5-6. That way, it can begin accepting work from our client.

```
C:\Users\thoma\OneDrive\!\Orleans\Apress\Solution\Introduction\Silo\bin\Debug\netcoreapp3.1\Silo.exe                    —    □    ✕
info: Orleans.Runtime.SiloLifecycleSubject[100452]
      Orleans.ClientLoggingHelper started in stage BecomeActive (19999) in 0.192 Milliseconds
info: Runtime.Messaging.GatewayClientCleanupAgent[0]
      Starting AsyncAgent Runtime.Messaging.GatewayClientCleanupAgent on managed thread 9
info: Orleans.Runtime.Silo[100452]
      Start gateway took 0 Milliseconds to finish
info: Orleans.Runtime.SiloLifecycleSubject[100452]
      Orleans.Runtime.Silo started in stage BecomeActive (19999) in 1.08 Milliseconds
info: Orleans.Runtime.MembershipService.MembershipTableManager[100645]
      ProcessTableUpdate (called from TryUpdateMyStatusGlobalOnce) membership table: 1 silos, 1 are Active, 0 are Dead,
Version=<2, 2>. All silos: [SiloAddress=S127.0.0.1:11111:363468510 SiloName=Silo_643b4 Status=Active]
info: Orleans.Runtime.MembershipService.MembershipAgent[100605]
      -Finished BecomeActive.
info: Orleans.Runtime.SiloLifecycleSubject[100452]
      MembershipAgent started in stage BecomeActive (19999) in 13.1216 Milliseconds
info: Orleans.Runtime.SiloLifecycleSubject[100452]
      Starting lifecycle stage BecomeActive (19999) took 13.1534 Milliseconds
info: Orleans.Runtime.SiloLifecycleSubject[100452]
      ClusterHealthMonitor started in stage Active (20000) in 0.1297 Milliseconds
info: Orleans.Runtime.SiloLifecycleSubject[100452]
      Orleans.Runtime.MembershipService.LocalSiloHealthMonitor started in stage Active (20000) in 0.1567 Milliseconds
info: Orleans.Runtime.SiloLifecycleSubject[100452]
      MembershipTableCleanupAgent started in stage Active (20000) in 0.1426 Milliseconds
info: Orleans.Runtime.SiloLifecycleSubject[100452]
      GatewayConnectionListener started in stage Active (20000) in 3.5107 Milliseconds
info: Orleans.Runtime.SiloLifecycleSubject[100452]
      Orleans.Runtime.Silo started in stage Active (20000) in 4.1689 Milliseconds
info: Orleans.Runtime.SiloLifecycleSubject[100452]
      Starting lifecycle stage Active (20000) took 6.928 Milliseconds
```

Figure 5-7. *Silo running. The silo is running and is active to begin taking work*

As shown in Figure 5-7, we can see that the silo has started and is in the active state. Now we are ready to start the client.

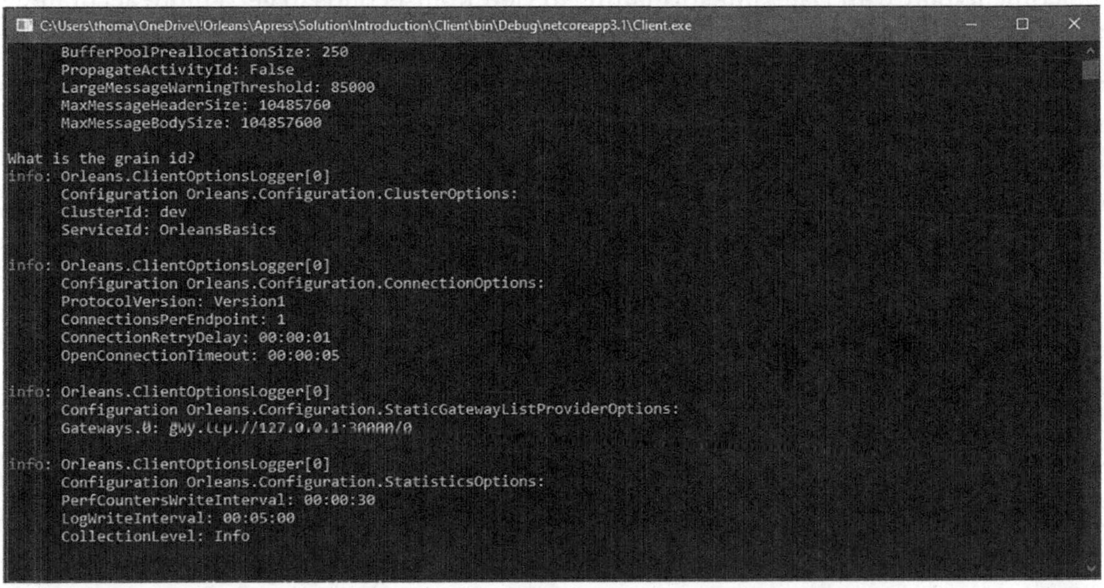

Figure 5-8. *Client running. The client is running and ready for our input. This is depicted by "What is the grain id?"*

2. We will want to start the client, as shown in Figure 5-8. Let the client load and connect to Orleans. *Note: Since the console is logging, the Console command requesting the grain name may not be at the bottom of the screen.

3. Enter any string that you prefer to name the grain, and a timestamp will be auto-appended.

4. Press Enter, and the message will be sent to Orleans, where a response will be generated. The grainId I used was "Test1".

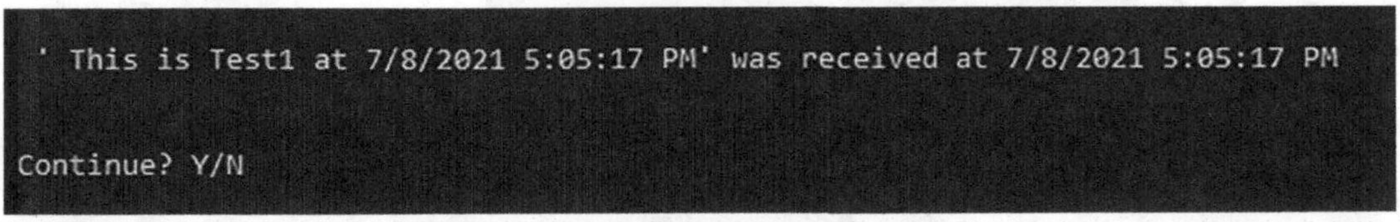

Figure 5-9. *Response. Display response from Orleans*

As we can see in Figure 5-9, a successful response is displayed. This is because GrainId – Test1 – was sent from the client and then received by the grain. You are welcome to play with DateTime formatting to view milliseconds to get a more accurate idea of the response time.

From this point forward, we can request to continue and enter additional or the same GrainIds. A response will be generated from that particular grain. Behind the scenes, the runtime is either activating a new grain or using an already active grain, which is dependent on the GrainId that is being requested.

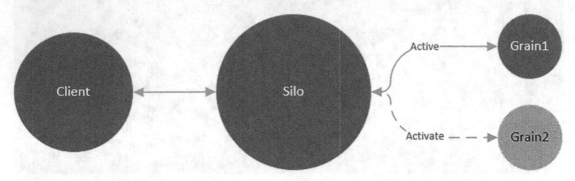

Figure 5-10. *Subsequent and new messages. Client messages request a specific grain*

What we see occurring, in Figure 5-10, is that the client is calling a specific GrainId. The runtime is aware that the grain is currently active (or in another state after creation) or needs to be created. If the grain is active, the message will be sent to the grain, and the response will be passed back to the client. If the grain hasn't been instantiated, it is activated and then performs the work returned to the client. This all occurs in very little time, and the lifecycle of the active grain is being orchestrated where it may be removed from memory by the time you call it again. Typically, it would be persisted in a database; however, we are not connected to a database for our local testing or this example.

Grain Communication

In addition to calling grains from the client, grains can communicate with one another as well. It is a foundational building block as we will step through it now. We will display how to test the communication in Chapter 7. When we invoke a call to another grain, we write it as if it is already active. If the grain isn't active, then the grain will be. This is all handled by the framework while removing the overhead from the developer.

We will set up another grain to see the following in action:

1. How grains can communicate

2. The ease of adding extending features

3. Intake of a string from the calling grain

4. Appending and returning an extended string

5. Setup for Chapter 7

We are creating a UnitTestingGrain to prepare for Chapter 7. We could just as easily extend the Tutorial grain; however, this book is about learning Orleans and gaining comfort with the framework, which takes reinforcement. So we will start by creating the UnitTestingGrain.

Setting Up the Testing Grain

We will create a new grain on our existing solution that we set up previously. Again, throughout this book, we will extend the initial solution as we would an actual application. I have attempted to name files of the completed solution for quick reference to assist in future Orleans development support.

Interface

1. We begin the process, just like we did in the beginning of this chapter.

    a. This time we are using the IGrainWithIntegerKey rather than IGrainWithString. We will see the grainId as 1 rather than "Test".

    The method accepts a string and returns a string.

IUnitTestingGrain

```
using System.Threading.Tasks;

namespace Introduction
{
    public interface IUnitTestingGrain : Orleans.IGrainWithIntegerKey
    {
        Task<string> ReturnMessageForTestAsync(string message);
    }
}
```

1. Next, we set up the grain based on our newly created interface.

    a. This grain will append "message: " to the string we send,
        allowing us to create a simple test to validate that the grain
        appends to our message as required.

UnitTestingGrain

```
using System;
using System.Collections.Generic;
using System.Text;
using System.Threading.Tasks;
using Introduction;
using Orleans;

namespace Introduction
{
    public class UnitTestingGrain : Orleans.Grain, IUnitTestingGrain
    {
        public Task<string> ReturnMessageForTestAsync(string message)
        {
            return Task.FromResult($"message: {message}");
        }
    }
}
```

Current solution state:

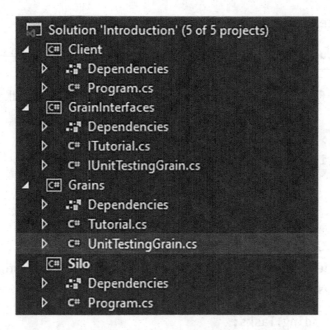

Figure 5-11. *Current solution. The grain and the interface have been added*

Currently, our solution should match Figure 5-11. We have added IUnitTestGrain.cs to the GrainInterfaces project. Also, we have added .cs to the Grains project. Now, we will have items to reference with the TestCluster.

Let's begin by adding a calling grain interface. We will set this grain up with a GUID key. It will

1. Receive an integer.

2. Store it locally (for testing purposes only; otherwise, it would be persisted).

3. Send it to the UnitTest grain.

4. Accept string response from UnitTest.

5. Return response.

ICallingGrain.cs

```csharp
using System.Threading.Tasks;

namespace Introduction
{
    public interface ICallingGrain : Orleans.IGrainWithGuidKey
    {
        Task<int> IncrementAsync(int number);
        Task<string> ReturnStringMessageAsync(int number);

    }
}
```

Create CallingGrain.cs

Next, we add the logic that increments the input, calls the UnitTestingGrain, and receives the response.

```csharp
using System.Threading.Tasks;
using Orleans;

namespace Introduction
{
    public class CallingGrain : Orleans.Grain, ICallingGrain
    {
        private int latest = 0;

        //increment the given number
        public Task<int> IncrementAsync(int number)
        {
            latest = number + 1;
            return Task.FromResult(latest);
        }

        public Task<string> ReturnStringMessageAsync(int number)
        {
            var grain = this.GrainFactory.GetGrain<IUnitTestingGrain>(1);
            return grain.ReturnMessageForTest(IncrementAsync(number).
            Result.ToString());
```

```
        }
    }
}
```

Update the Silo

After creating the testing and calling grains, we can add them to the silo where we register them with the silo IoC. The additional code is added to the Silo.Program.cs StartSilo method as seen in the following:

```
private static async Task<ISiloHost> StartSilo()
{
    // define the cluster configuration
    var builder = new SiloHostBuilder()
        .UseLocalhostClustering()
        .ConfigureApplicationParts(parts => parts.AddFrom
        ApplicationBaseDirectory())
        .Configure<ClusterOptions>(options =>
        {
            options.ClusterId = "dev";
            options.ServiceId = "OrleansBasics";
        })
        .ConfigureApplicationParts(parts => parts.AddApplication
        Part(typeof(TutorialGrain).Assembly).WithReferences())
        .ConfigureApplicationParts(parts => parts.AddApplication
        Part(typeof(UnitTestingGrain).Assembly).WithReferences())
        .ConfigureApplicationParts(parts => parts.AddApplication
        Part(typeof(CallingGrain).Assembly).WithReferences())
        .ConfigureLogging(logging => logging.AddConsole());

    var host = builder.Build();

    await host.StartAsync();
    return host;
}
```

If you choose to extend the console application to correspond with the CallingGrain, you will receive the appended message.

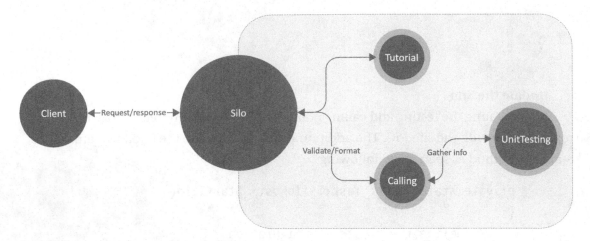

Figure 5-12. *Current setup. The current flow of our application*

After the latest code implementation in the silo, we can now make calls from the client and to the Tutorial, Calling, and UnitTesting grains. Since we have already established how to collect the client to call an Orleans grain, it is an optional task to do so for our project. The Calling and UnitTesting grains were established to show how grains call and respond to one another while also setting the stage for unit testing. As of now, we will refer to Figure 5-12 as our current flow.

Summary

In this chapter, we covered the creation of a base project and saw Orleans in action. The projects

- *Silo* – Runtime and references the grains

- *Client* – Makes calls to Orleans silo to request work

- *Grains* – Virtual actors that do the work

- *GrainInterfaces* – Grain abstractions

- *Grain communication*

were added to a single solution for local development. We set up the interface, then the grain, then the silo, and finally the client. GrainInterfaces are required project references of all of the projects, while Grains only need to be referenced by Silo.

We deleted the default classes in Grains and GrainInterfaces and then added the NuGet packages to appropriate projects. This allowed us to start adding code. First, we started with the interface since it will define the grain method(s) and be used in the client. Then we created the StringKey grain, which appends a timestamp and returns the message. Afterward, the silo was built for local development and referenced our newly created grain. Finally, we coded the client where the user is prompted for a grainId where Orleans will send the message to the particular grain and return a message to the console.

The process was then reviewed to show that the grainId may call an active grain or create a new one, based on the id requested. It also helps us understand the lifecycle of the grain, such as if you wait long enough, the grain will be removed from memory and reactivated on request.

We added the Calling and UnitTesting grains to showcase intergrain communication. It is very east to set up and is a setup in Chapter 7. Currently, we have a client that will call the silo, which returns info from the Tutorial grain. As an optional task, you are able to extend the client to call the Calling and UnitTesting grains. These can be set up in the same manner in which we created the initial client call.

In the next chapter, we will learn about timers and reminders. The timers will be another item added to unit testing. Both timers and reminders are great for handling repeating tasks.

CHAPTER 6

Timers and Reminders

Overview

There are many scenarios where we would need to use reoccurring calls. For instance, we may need to connect to another service every few seconds to pull the latest information, such as for stock prices to display them to the users, or we might be building our own health monitoring service. In these scenarios, we would either rely on the cloud platform or a third-party application or create our own that triggers the process at specific intervals.

Luckily, Orleans created timers and reminders to do just that. We can set up timers and reminders to kick off events at specific intervals. Most solutions requiring a timer will usually need to set this up through our cloud platform, host a third-party application, or build our own. We do not need to set up external tools for our application, including the persistence, to use this feature. We must note that there is a primary difference between timers and reminders.

Timer lifetimes are not persisted beyond the life of the grain or if there is a cluster failure. They work perfectly for updates of page feeds such as scoreboards and stocks. Also, they are disposable, so they can be turned off when they are no longer needed and the resources can be returned. This means that they do not outlive the life of the grain or the cluster. Timers made to tackle shorter time spans by running in smaller intervals, such as in seconds or minutes.

What if we need a reoccurring action to take place even if there is a failure? Reminders are persisted in a database and will continue once they are restarted. Reminders will need to be turned off when needed, because they live outside the cluster's lifetime. Since they are persisted, they are seen after a new instance has replaced the failed cluster. Reminders, unlike timers, are not built to run as frequently, where we are using intervals of minutes, hours, or days. It removes the need to start each

© Thomas Nelson 2022

T. Nelson, *Introducing Microsoft Orleans*, https://doi.org/10.1007/978-1-4842-8014-0_6

timer through code, or other means, after an issue. This eliminates the need for us to keep a list of every timer that needs to be started again or to be concerned about failures not starting events since it would be automatically start.

So why are both timers and reminders created? It's because the tools are created to meet the need of the specific requirement. Not all timed calls need to be stored in the database --like calls during sessions--, and others do meet that need, such as report generation. A benefit of using these is items come from using them together when needed. The reminders can be used to start the timers. We can view the reminders, in this perspective, as a single point of orchestration to kick off the timers that may have stopped due to a failure.

In this chapter, we are going to create both a timer and a reminder. The timer will return a sequential count based on a set interval. The reminder will be set up, with and without a database. Don't worry; we will walk through setting up Azure tables in an optional section to expose you to the local development setup and how the application works in a more realistic structure.

Creating a Timer

Let's begin. Timers are easy to add to our solution. Our timer will be activated by the client and will then display each time it runs. We are also able to stop the timer through the client. We start just as we have with our other grains by implementing the interface.

ITimerGrain.cs is created in the GrainInterfaces project.

```
namespace Introduction
{
    public interface ITimerGrain : Orleans.IGrainWithGuidKey
    {
        void StartTimer();
        void StopTimer();
    }
}
```

We are adding the ability to start and stop the timer as needed. Timers are disposables we will see in the class.

TimerGrain.cs is created in the Grains project.

```csharp
using System;
using System.Threading.Tasks;

namespace Introduction
{
    public class TimerGrain : Orleans.Grain, ITimerGrain
    {
        private IDisposable _timer;

        public void StartTimer()
        {
            Console.WriteLine($"Timer Started {DateTime.Now}");
        }

        public void StopTimer()
        {
            _timer.Dispose();
            Console.WriteLine($"Timer Stopped {DateTime.Now}");
        }

        public override Task OnActivateAsync()
        {
            int count = 1;

            _timer = RegisterTimer(state =>
            {
                Console.WriteLine($"Timer number: {count}");
                count++;
                return base.OnActivateAsync();
            }, null,
            TimeSpan.FromSeconds(3),
                TimeSpan.FromSeconds(2));

            return base.OnActivateAsync();
        }
    }
}
```

The TimerGrain class will display when the timer starts and stops. As mentioned previously, we dispose of the timer to stop it. The timer displays "Timer number: " along with a sequential counting of the timer execution. We are adding the function to the state and are not passing a parameter, so we use null. Then, the initial run of the function will start after 3 seconds and then will continue at the frequency of every 2 seconds.

Now, we update our existing client to start and stop the timer as needed.

Client Program.cs's DoClientWork is updated to activate and dispose of the trigger.

```
private static async Task DoClientWork(IClusterClient client)
{
    bool repeat = true;
    bool timerStarted = false;
    ITimerGrain timer = null;

    Console.WriteLine("Start timer Grain? Y/N");
    if (Console.ReadLine()?.ToUpper() == "Y")
    {
        timer = client.GetGrain<ITimerGrain>(Guid.Empty);
        timer.StartTimer();
        timerStarted = true;
    }

    do
    {
        // Grain Identity
        Console.WriteLine("What is the grain id?");
        string grainId = Console.ReadLine();

        // Call Specific Grain
        var example = client.GetGrain<ITutorialGrain>(grainId);

        // Send Message with time stamp
        var response = await example.RespondWIthCurrentTime
        ($" This is {grainId} at {DateTime.Now}");

        // View response
        Console.WriteLine($"\n\n{response}\n\n");
```

```
            // Continue the example
            Console.WriteLine("Continue? Y/N");
            string continueResponse = Console.ReadLine();

            if (continueResponse.ToUpper() == "N")
            {
                repeat = false;
            }

            if (timerStarted)
            {
                // Continue Timer
                Console.WriteLine("Continue Timer? Y/N");

                if (Console.ReadLine()?.ToUpper() == "N")
                {
                    timer.StopTimer();
                    timerStarted = false;
                }
            }

        } while (repeat);

        return;
    }
}
```

The client gives the option to start the timer and when to stop it. It will continuously run until we stop it or the cluster.

Running the Timer

Run the silo and then the client. The client console will request input to start the timer, as shown in Figure 6-1. Type "Y" and press Enter to activate the timer.

```
Start timer Grain? Y/N
```

Figure 6-1. *Start timer input. Do we start the timer?*

```
Timer Started 9/25/2021 9:00:34 PM
Timer number: 1
Timer number: 2
Timer number: 3
Timer number: 4
Timer number: 5
Timer number: 6
Timer number: 7
Timer number: 8
Timer number: 9
Timer number: 10
Timer number: 11
```

Figure 6-2. *Active timer. The timer is running and displaying actions.*

You will see the timer starting in the silo console as seen above in Figure 6-2. The initial call date and time are recorded. From that point forward, the timer will execute, and the counter will sequentially grow. We can watch this grow until we stop the silo or decide to stop the timer.

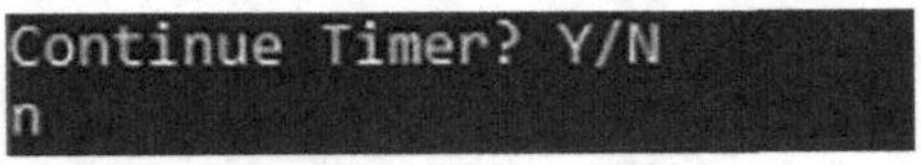

```
Continue Timer? Y/N
n
```

Figure 6-3. *Stopping the timer. Client console stopping the time timer*

The client console will ask if you would like to continue the timer. Type "N" and press Enter as depicted in Figure 6-3. The response will activate the stop method and stop the timer by disposing of it.

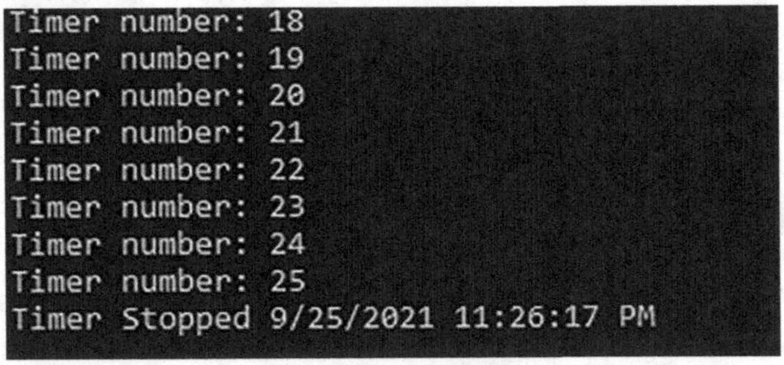

```
Timer number: 18
Timer number: 19
Timer number: 20
Timer number: 21
Timer number: 22
Timer number: 23
Timer number: 24
Timer number: 25
Timer Stopped 9/25/2021 11:26:17 PM
```

Figure 6-4. *Timer stopped. The timer is stopped.*

When we enter "N," then "Timer Stopped" will display on the silo console that is shown in Figure 6-4. Implementing a timer is very easy and extremely helpful. Next, we will create a reminder that is persisted in a database.

Creating a Reminder

Reminders take a little bit more effort to implement since we need a database. First, we will walk through how to add the reminder with an in-memory placeholder. Then we will set up an Azure table and store our reminder.

Program.cs is in the Silo project.

We need to add the in-memory placeholder in the StartSilo method. This allows us to set up a reminder without the use of a database. We will set up a database after this section to show how the tools interact. Add the code in bold to StartSilo:

```
private static async Task<ISiloHost> StartSilo()
{
    // define the cluster configuration
    var builder = new SiloHostBuilder()
        .UseLocalhostClustering()
        .ConfigureApplicationParts(parts => parts.
        AddFromApplicationBaseDirectory())
        .Configure<ClusterOptions>(options =>
        {
            options.ClusterId = "dev";
            options.ServiceId = "OrleansBasics";
        })
        .ConfigureApplicationParts(parts => parts.AddApplicationPart
        (typeof(TutorialGrain).Assembly).WithReferences())
        .ConfigureApplicationParts(parts => parts.AddApplicationPart
        (typeof(UnitTestingGrain).Assembly).WithReferences())
        .ConfigureApplicationParts(parts => parts.AddApplicationPart
        (typeof(CallingGrain).Assembly).WithReferences())
        .ConfigureApplicationParts(parts => parts.AddApplicationPart
        (typeof(TimerGrain).Assembly).WithReferences())
```

```
            .UseInMemoryReminderService()
            .ConfigureLogging(logging => logging.AddConsole());

        var host = builder.Build();

        await host.StartAsync();
        return host;
    }
```

Next, we set up the interface.

IReminderGrain.cs is added to the GrainInterfaces project.

```
using System.Threading.Tasks;
using Orleans;

namespace GrainInterfaces
{
    public interface IReminderGrain : IGrainWithStringKey, IRemindable
    {
        Task SendMessage();
        Task StopMessage();
    }
}
```

IReminderGrain is set up like the timer by including a start and stop function. Additionally, we add IRemindable as an additional interface.

ReminderGrain.cs is created under the Grains project.

```
using System;
using System.Threading.Tasks;
using GrainInterfaces;
using Orleans;
using Orleans.Providers;
using Orleans.Runtime;

namespace Introduction
{
    public class ReminderGrain : Orleans.Grain, IReminderGrain
    {
```

```
const string ReminderName = "reminderMessage";

//Work to perform
public Task ReceiveReminder(string reminderName, TickStatus status)
{
    //Determine if it matches the name of the reminder
    if (reminderName == ReminderName)
    {
        Console.WriteLine($"Reminder message created at:
        {DateTime.Now}");
    }
     return Task.CompletedTask;
}

//Register the reminder; starting in 30 min and 1 hour thereafter
public Task SendMessage()
{
    return RegisterOrUpdateReminder(ReminderName, TimeSpan.
    FromMinutes(30), TimeSpan.FromHours(1));
}
//Unregister the reminder
public async Task StopMessage()
{
    foreach (var reminder in await GetReminders())
    {
        if (reminder.ReminderName == ReminderName)
        {
            await UnregisterReminder(reminder);
        }
    }
}
    }
}
```

Setting Up an Azure Table

Azure is not required for Orleans as it is cloud agnostic and is being used as an example. If you do not have an Azure account, you can sign up for a free account here: https://azure.microsoft.com/en-us/free.

Once you have an account, sign in to the account. We need to set up a storage account to use the Azure table.

We start by clicking the hamburger menu, as shown in Figure 6-5. A list of items will be displayed.

Figure 6-5. *Azure menu. Hamburger menu to create a new resource*

Figure 6-6 displays the expanded menu. We click "Create a resource" to pull up the resource Marketplace. Marketplace is a collection of all of the Azure and third-party toolsets.

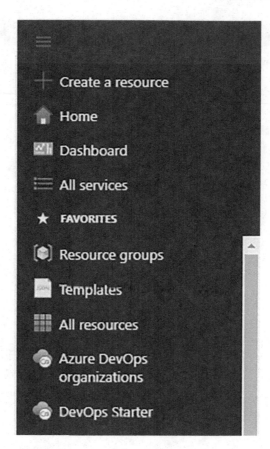

Figure 6-6. *Azure menu items*

Marketplace has a search bar through which we will want to look up "storage account." As shown in Figure 6-7, Storage account is our first result. Click the "Storage account" result.

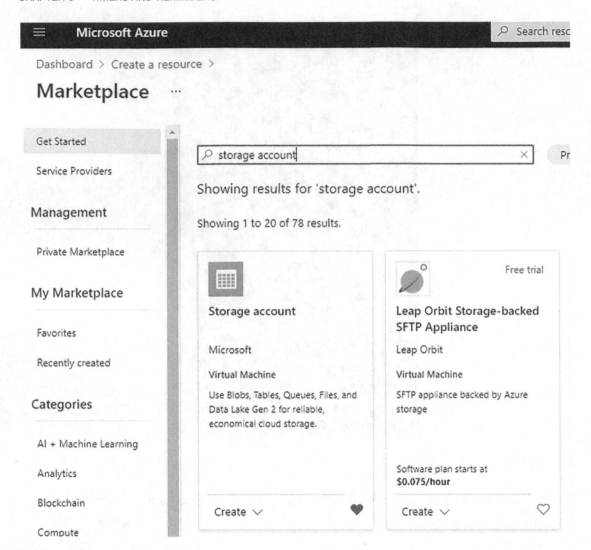

Figure 6-7. *Storage account. Search results for resources*

The page, as shown in Figure 6-8, will display information about the storage account. We can check the plans ahead of time. We want to click "Create."

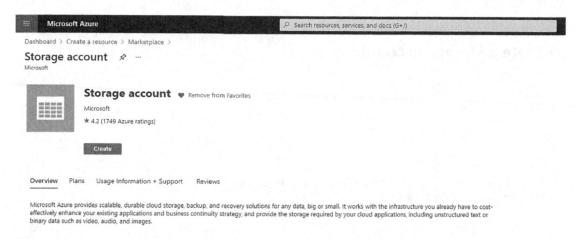

Figure 6-8. *Select Storage account. Select Storage account to set up the storage account.*

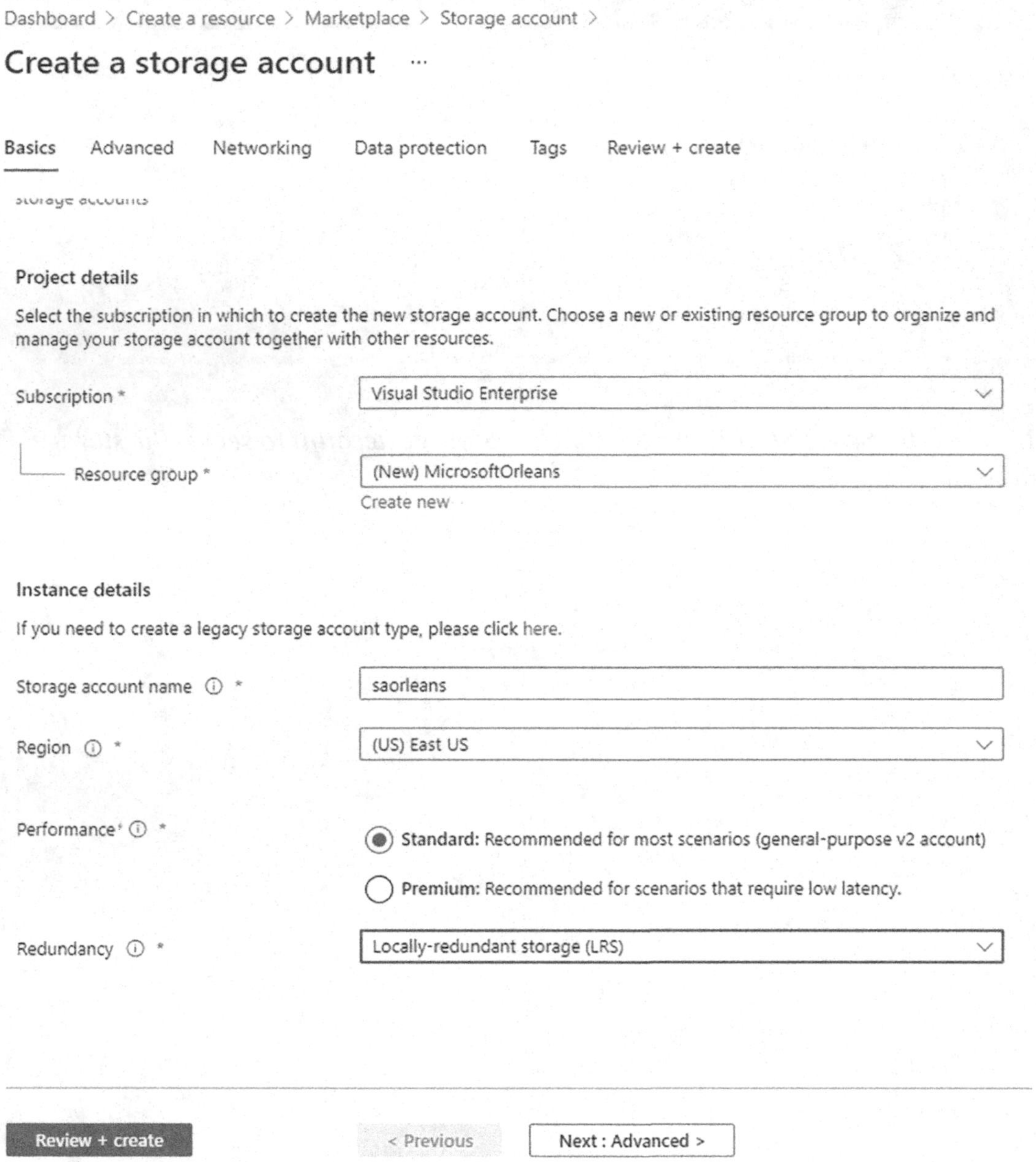

Dashboard > Create a resource > Marketplace > Storage account >

Create a storage account ···

Basics   Advanced   Networking   Data protection   Tags   Review + create

storage accounts

Project details

Select the subscription in which to create the new storage account. Choose a new or existing resource group to organize and manage your storage account together with other resources.

Subscription *	Visual Studio Enterprise ⌄

Resource group *	(New) MicrosoftOrleans ⌄

Create new

Instance details

If you need to create a legacy storage account type, please click here.

Storage account name ⓘ *	saorleans

Region ⓘ *	(US) East US ⌄

Performance⁺ ⓘ *   ⦿ **Standard:** Recommended for most scenarios (general-purpose v2 account)

⚪ **Premium:** Recommended for scenarios that require low latency.

Redundancy ⓘ *	Locally-redundant storage (LRS) ⌄

[Review + create]   < Previous   Next : Advanced >

Figure 6-9. *Storage setup*

Your subscription may be pay-per-use, which is fine. I created a new resource group that logically groups resources together.

The storage account is named "saorleans" and is based in the East US region as shown in Figure 6-9. Choose the region close to you to cut down latency.

We will use a standard setup with local redundancy for this example.

It will take a few moments for the resource to build and then become available. This is because we are waiting for Azure to create the storage on a server and then set up the network, which is then made available for us. Once the storage is available for use, click "Go to resource," as shown in Figure 6-10.

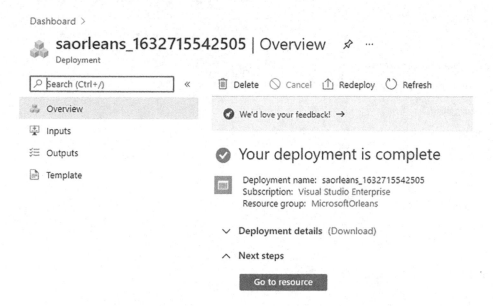

Figure 6-10. *Deployment completion*

In Figure 6-11, we can see that the resource has been created, and now we can create our table. Click the blade named Tables, and you will see the menu that allows us to make our Azure table. In the newly loaded menu, click "+ Table." This will load the menu for us to implement an Azure table. I named the table tblorleans as shown in Figure 6-12.

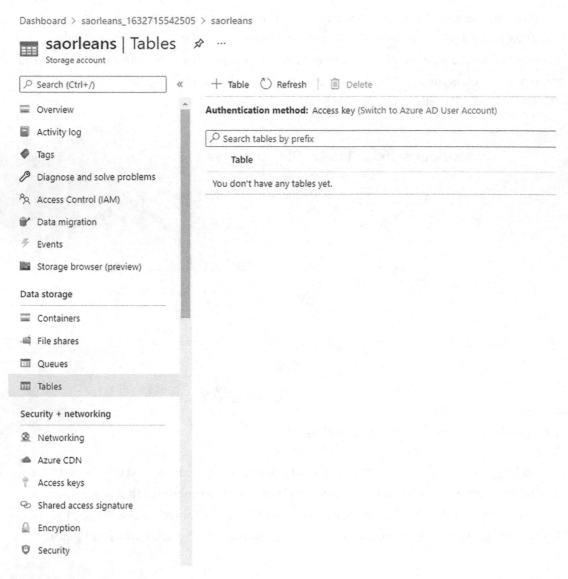

Figure 6-11. *Tables blade*

Figure 6-12. *Adding a table*

Once the table has been created, we will need to get the connection string to add it to our application. Click the Access keys blade. As shown in Figure 6-13, we want to click Show keys and then copy the connection string from either key1 or key2. They will both work. We are given two passwords because we can scope where they are used to minimize an outage in a security breach.

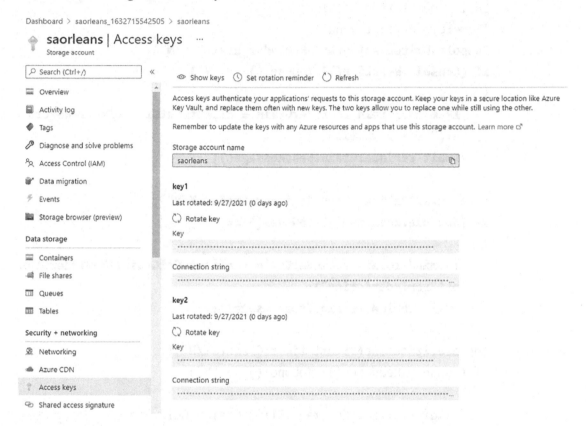

Figure 6-13. *Access keys*

To connect this to our silo, we would replace ".UseInMemoryReminderService()" with ".UseAzureTableReminderService(options => options.ConnectionString = connectionString)". This will make the connection to the storage that we created and persist the reminder(s). We will not pursue this any longer as it delves further into cloud development and will cloud Chapter 9. This is a perfect opportunity to extend the project.

Running the Reminder

Now that the reminder is set up, we need to initiate it. We need to update the client to call the register and unregister methods. We do this by adding the code in bold to the DoClientWork method in the Client project.

Program.cs

```
private static async Task DoClientWork(IClusterClient client)
    {
        bool repeat = true;
        bool timerStarted = false;
        ITimerGrain timer = null;
        Console.WriteLine("Start Reminder Grain? Y/N");
        if (Console.ReadLine()?.ToUpper() == "Y")
        {
            IReminderGrain reminderGrain = client.GetGrain<IReminderGrai
            n>("reminderAction");
            await reminderGrain.SendMessage();
        }
        Console.WriteLine("Stop Reminder Grain? Y/N");
        if (Console.ReadLine()?.ToUpper() == "Y")
        {
            IReminderGrain reminderGrain = client.GetGrain<IReminderGrai
            n>("reminderAction");
            await reminderGrain.StopMessage();
        }
        Console.WriteLine("Start timer Grain? Y/N");
        if (Console.ReadLine()?.ToUpper() == "Y")
        {
            timer = client.GetGrain<ITimerGrain>(Guid.Empty);
            timer.StartTimer();
            timerStarted = true;
        }
        do
        {
            // Grain Identity
            Console.WriteLine("What is the grain id?");
            string grainId = Console.ReadLine();
            // Call Specific Grain
            var example = client.GetGrain<ITutorialGrain>(grainId);

            //Send Message with time stamp
```

```
var response = await example.RespondWIthCurrentTime
                ($" This is {grainId} at {DateTime.Now}");
//View response
Console.WriteLine($"\n\n{response}\n\n");
//Continue the example
Console.WriteLine("Continue? Y/N");
string continueResponse = Console.ReadLine();
if (continueResponse.ToUpper() == "N")
{
    repeat = false;
}
if (timerStarted)
{
    //Continue Timer
    Console.WriteLine("Continue Timer? Y/N");
    if (Console.ReadLine()?.ToUpper() == "N")
    {
        timer.StopTimer();
        timerStarted = false;
    }
}
} while (repeat);
return;
}
```

Now we can run the projects again. We work through the command-line requests. Type "Y" to start the reminder. You can cycle through the commands to stop the reminder as well. Feel free to challenge yourself and connect the reminder to a database. Then query the database to view the records that Orleans stores.

- AddMemoryGrainStorage – Grain state will be kept in memory and probably will be lost when the machine is down or a new version is deployed.

- AddAzureBlobGrainStorage – Azure Blob Storage will be used.

- AddAzureTableGrainStorage – Azure Table API will be used. Cosmos DB Table API is also compatible but is beyond the need of this tutorial.

- AddAdoNetGrainStorage – ADO.Net storage in MSSQL database.

- AddDynamoDBGrainStorage – Amazon AWS DynamoDB storage.

Summary

We covered a lot in this chapter. We started with the differences between timers and reminders, which primarily revolve around the life span. Timers do not outlive the life of a cluster and do not require a database for production use. However, they will not start again automatically, only once the unhealthy cluster is replaced with a healthy cluster and retriggered.

On the other hand, reminders are persisted in a database and will continue running after a failure. This removes the need to start up and maintain a list of each timer to restart. It is a useful pattern to have reminders call timers momentarily so that in the case of an event, the reminders will momentarily restart the timers. This will minimize unforeseen downtime of specific aspects of the application.

We kicked off the project by adding a timer. Then, we added an interface with starting and stopping actions, disposing of the timer when it is no longer needed. In the timer code, we added the action and then the intermittent time frames. Remember, the time frames do NOT include the time it takes to execute the function itself. In the first time span, it is the wait time before the initial execution. The second time span is the wait between each event after that. For instance, we can wait 30 minutes after the initial call timer and then run every 5 minutes after that.

Our initial implementation of reminders was stored in memory, UseInMemoryReminderService, for development purposes. Then we walked through how to create an Azure table to persist our reminder. To do so, we used the UseAzureTablesReminderService and appended the connection string. We are not tied to using these forms of storage, and it can be hosted outside of Azure.

Finally, we ran our project and ran our grain. Again, we were able to see the result validating that the reminder was working as expected, which is a nice ending for the chapter. However, you can take it a step further. As mentioned earlier, you can have the reminder call a timer to restart it if there is a cluster failure. Then it will start them without you having to make the calls to the timers to start them. Another Reminder setup can be found here: https://kritner.medium.com/microsoft-orleans-reminders-and-grains-calling-grains-6ad58ad104a2. Also, this is a wonderful video of Timers and Reminders: https://www.youtube.com/watch?v=SKI_YUMSqgM. This will give you more items to add to your toolbox as we as we dive further into the framework.

## CHAPTER 7

Unit Tests

As with any software, we need to test it. Thankfully, a NuGet library allows us to set up a host to run our unit tests. This chapter will set up a grain to test, a unit test project, test the code, and execute the test. Also, we will learn about Orleans' TestingHost while setting up xUnit's testing framework that runs grains on a silo stood up specifically for testing. We will learn how to test individual methods, call grains, and test the response from a grain called. I enjoy setting up tests for my code and enjoy the way unit tests are support by Orleans.

This chapter is essential to understand, so that the software can be tested as it is being built. Test-Driven Development (TDD) is not a new pattern, and luckily we can use the ability to incorporate it with Orleans development. Otherwise, we would have to wait until DevOps pipelines are set up and functional/end-to-end testing is added. This allows us to be proactive in error correction and a decent comfort level when extending the application.

We will not cover TDD best practices but are focusing on a unit test implementation. It is commonly debated that the tests should be created before the tested methods, which require us to run the tests as we write the code. It is a more streamlined approach that reduces refactoring. I use this technique myself when the outcome is known. Unfortunately, this is not always an available option, such as when we are experimenting with code. After experimenting and once I feel comfortable with the logic, I will set up the unit tests to validate my results. In either case, we should end our development cycle with working unit tests. It allows us to build on top of working code and be alert if additional features cause unexpected outcomes in existing logic.

Unit Test Summary

I have given presentations supporting unit testing and been involved in several unit test debates when working in my previous positions. Unit tests are an excellent way to prove that our work is providing the expected value. In traditional TDD, we write the tests first and then write our desired outcome. It is ran to fail the first time and then ran after that to get the results that we are expecting. This is not the tactic that we are

© Thomas Nelson 2022
T. Nelson, *Introducing Microsoft Orleans*, https://doi.org/10.1007/978-1-4842-8014-0_7

taking in the book. Instead, we are discovering various items that are needed for our project and how to implement them.

Before we start, let's talk about the usefulness of unit tests. Some companies base success metrics on the percentage of project test coverage. My personal preference is to have strong unit tests that cover core and extended features. Suppose, for a moment, that unit test coverage percentages or defining quality tests is being discussed as a standard at your company. Would you side with breadth or quality, not that they can't be intertwined. In either case, it needs to be understood that the threshold being mandated directly relates to the overhead of the development team. A comfortable required percentage has generally been 70–80% coverage if you choose to use percentages, but percentages do not capture *what* is being tested. Choosing core and extended methods might be a better practice depending on your company's success metrics.

What can unit tests do for us? As we build our applications, unit tests prove that the work has been done correctly. They prove methods work as we write them. Since they are have an atomic scope, they are easily written as we develop. Also, as we continue to write them, we can show proof that our work has been completed and expected.

Also, they are used in pipelines as we build the solution for deployment. They will run after building the application and fail the rest of the deployment if an error is found. Also, the percentage amount can be used to determine if the test coverage is adequate to be deployed through automation. These are quantitative items that can be used in pipelines to determine if code is suitable for deployment.

Unit tests also allow us to determine if new items added to the code affect the results of the existing code. For instance, imagine an application that we have already written, and additional features are required. These features might affect the current application, where if unit tests were not added, we would need to wait for functional tests to be ran. This can severely impact the delivery time which can compound, like interest rates, the software cycle exponentially with technical debt. Having the unit tests in place reduces the delivery time by knowing if the code negatively impacts the previous code. This substantially decreases technical debt since we know it is working properly.

Orleans Unit Testing Overview

To set up the unit tests for Orleans, we will need to set up xUnit. xUnit can set up a cluster fixture, which is our testing cluster. It allows us to have complete control over the testing cluster. This will come in handy when various grains need to be registered with the clusters, such as fake timers and reminders.

Several items can be overridden in the grain so we can set them up in the test cluster. These items are outside the scope of this book since they are relatively complicated and dig deeper into xUnit and more advanced features of Orleans internals.

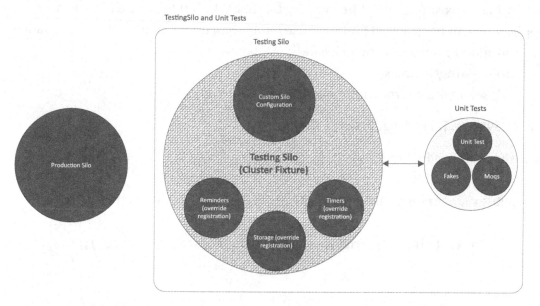

Figure 7-1. *Testing silo and unit tests. Testing silo separation from production silo and unit testing*

Thanks to the TestingHost NuGet package, we can create a separate silo that can be configured and manipulated for testing purposes. As shown in Figure 7-1, the production silo is separated entirely from the testing. This allows us to change the testing silo set up to test the grains as required. This includes the ability to set up timers, reminders, fake storage, and so on. That way, we don't have to manipulate our grains or add workaround code that may harm the application from execution to maintenance.The unit tests are set up very much in the same manner as traditional tests. We create the instance and use its methods. We can use fakes and moqs to create grains and use them to call one another to validate the results. The only caveat is that depending on the test, we may need to override specific items in the grains to be overwritten by the test case.

To summarize specifically what is happening in Figure 7-1, the testing silo is set up as the runtime for us to use as needed against the unit tests. The unit tests will instantiate the grains or moqs of the grains based on the testing needs. This shields the actual silo from any possible harm by residing outside of the testing domain.

Creating Our Unit Test Grain

To walk through this, we will create a new testing grain to see the setup instead of modifying an existing grain. When writing this book, I want to ensure that the final application can be reviewed for future use rather than updated items that may change the information you are trying to locate.

IUnitTestingGrain.cs

Let's set up the interface for the test grain:

```
using System.Threading.Tasks;

namespace Introduction
{
    public interface IUnitTestingGrain : Orleans.IGrainWithIntegerKey
    {
        Task<string> ReturnMessageForTestAsync(string message);
    }
}
```

This grain will accept a message and return a message. We will confirm the returned message.

UnitTestingGrain.cs

Then we set up the grain as seen in the following:

```
using System.Threading.Tasks;

namespace Introduction
{
    public class UnitTestingGrain : Orleans.Grain, IUnitTestingGrain
    {
        public async Task<string> ReturnMessageForTestAsync(string message)
        {
            return await Task.FromResult($"message: {message}");
        }
    }
}
```

The unit test grain accepts a string and will append "message: ". This is a straightforward example of walking us through the process.

Setting Up Our Test Cluster

1. Next, we will set up a testing project named UnitTests. We will use this project to implement xUnit in conjunction with TestingHost to build the tests. This setup allows us to use the same TestingHost throughout the testing needs, rather than on an individual test basis.

2. Add the following NuGet packages for the testing project:

   a. xUnit

   b. Microsoft.Orleans.TestingHost

3. Add a project reference to our GrainInterfaces and Grains projects.

4. Next, we will create the additional classes and add the code for our testing. We will start with the class that performs the tests and the supporting classes that run the cluster once per test runner rather than per test. *Note: The supportive classes are stored in a folder named TestingCluster.

UnitTest.cs

```
using System.Threading.Tasks;
using GrainInterfaces;
using Orleans.TestingHost;
using xUnit;

namespace UnitTests
{
    [Collection(ClusterCollection.Name)]
    public class UnitGrainTest
    {
        private readonly TestCluster _cluster;
```

```
    public UnitGrainTest(ClusterFixture fixture)
    {
        _cluster = fixture.Cluster;
    }

    [Fact]
    public async Task IsMessageCorrectAsync()
    {
        string message = "Test";

        var test = _cluster.GrainFactory.GetGrain<I>(1);
        var result = await test.ReturnMessageForTest(message);

        string expected = $"message: {message}";
        Assert.Equal(expected, result);
    }
  }
}
```

The UnitTests class is where we do our testing logic, as we see in the IsMessageCorrectAsync. We store our message and then pass it to the test cluster, initializing our grain from the interface.

Also, there are a couple of lines that we haven't delved into and will be used throughout Orleans. First, we instantiate the grain, and then we make a call to it. These are commonly used throughout Orleans, and we will see it later in this chapter as we call a grain from another grain. *Note: This is a repetitive baseline pattern.

1. `var grain = this.GrainFactory.GetGrain<IUnitTesting Grain>(1);`

    a. The grain is instantiated from the GrainFactory, which is based on the interface of the UnitTestingGrain.

2. `return grain.ReturnMessageForTest(IncrementAsync(number). Result.ToString());`

    a. The instantiated grain is then used to make the call and return the response.

ClusterFixture.cs

```
using Orleans.TestingHost;
using System;

public class ClusterFixture : IDisposable
{
    public ClusterFixture()
    {
        var builder = new TestClusterBuilder();
        // Setting up TestSiloConfigurations allows us to configure silos
        in the cluster
        //builder.AddSiloBuilderConfigurator<TestSiloConfigurations>();
        this.Cluster = builder.Build();
        this.Cluster.Deploy();
    }

    public void Dispose()
    {
        this.Cluster.StopAllSilos();
    }

    public TestCluster Cluster { get; private set; }
}
```

The fixture allows us to use the cluster across multiple test cases (Candeias, 2019). The commented code that contains the TestSiloConfiguration will enable us to configure silos in the test cluster.

ClusterCollection.cs

```
using xUnit;

namespace UnitTests
{
    [CollectionDefinition(ClusterCollection.Name)]
    public class ClusterCollection : ICollectionFixture<ClusterFixture>
    {
        public const string Name = "Chapter6UnitTesting";
    }
}
```

ClusterCollection completes the fixture for use to reuse the cluster across the tests.

Optional: TestSiloConfigurations.cs

```
using System;
using System.Collections.Generic;
using System.Text;
using Microsoft.Extensions.DependencyInjection;
using Orleans.Hosting;
using Orleans.TestingHost;

namespace UnitTests
{
    public class TestSiloConfigurations : ISiloBuilderConfigurator
    {
        public void Configure(ISiloHostBuilder hostBuilder)
        {
            hostBuilder.ConfigureServices(services =>
            {
                // Services that need to talk to grains can be placed here
                services.AddSingleton<IService, Service>();
            });
        }
    }
}
```

TestSiloConfiguration can be passed into the ClusterFixture through the builder. AddSiloBuilderConfigurator. We will not cover the implementation; however, it should be reviewed for possible future needs. You can find more information here: https://dotnet.github.io/orleans/docs/tutorials_and_samples/testing.html?q=TestSilo Configuration.

Running the Test(s)

We can run tests just as we have in any other application. The test runner detects the tests and executes them. I have noticed that it takes a short moment for the TestSilo to initialize before the unit test execution.

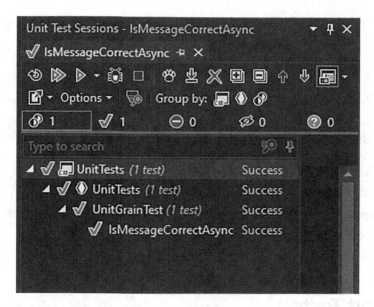

Figure 7-2. *Test runner. Successful test outcome*

We can see in Figure 7-2 that the test was found and executed successfully. In addition, we can see that these tests are run in the same manner as any other service. These allow us to test specific outcomes of code within the grain. What about how grains interact together? How are we able to see messages that are passed? Then, we can set them up to run just as they would in the typical silo!

Adding the CallingGrain Test

We can ensure that the messages sent from a grain are working correctly and return the expected information. It is straightforward to do with TestingHost, as it will activate the grains and make the calls as usual. Also, we will expand our UnitTest grain to house the latest result. Then we will set up the tests to run and verify the results.

Our calling grain is set up and receives the message from our UnitTestingGrain, in theory. Next, we need to prove our code to make sure it calls correctly and responds as expected. Open UnitTest.cs, and let's add an additional test.

```
[Fact]
public async Task TestGrainCommunication()
{
    // instantiate the grain
```

```
        var grain = _cluster.GrainFactory.GetGrain<ICallingGrain>
                (Guid.Empty);

        // make calling grain
        var result = await grain.ReturnStringMessageAsync(1); mock
        // validate the response of the calling grain
        Assert.Equal("message: 2", result);
    }
```

In the preceding code, we instantiated the test grain with a Guid grain identity. Then we called the method that gathers a response from UnitTestingGrain. Finally, we validate whether the expected outcome is appending "message: " and that the input has been incremented from 1 to 2.

Run the Unit Tests

The unit tests will prove that the grains are being instantiated and are correctly communicating.

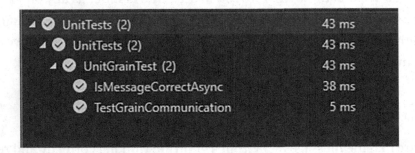

Figure 7-3. *Test runner. The successful outcome of both tests*

After running the tests, you should see passing results. Figure 7-3 shows us that both the UnitTestingGrain IsMessageCorrectAsync and TestGrainCommunication methods are working as expected. Great job!

Also, we can add moqs by adding the Moq NuGet package, found here: `https://www.nuget.org/packages/Moq`. Moqs allow us to return a specific result without calling the actual instance. For example, perhaps the grain is calling a database or has been tested by other means, and we want to validate specific responses that is without relying on external connections.

They are implemented, as shown in Orleans' documentation, as simple as

```
var mockedGrain = new Mock<IMockedGrain>();
```

We can have the mockedGrain return information by overriding the GrainFactory to verify that the mockedGrain interacts with otherGrain.

```
var otherGrain = new Mock<IOtherGrain>();
otherGrain.Setup(x => x.GrainFactory.GetGrain<IMockedGrain>(It.
IsAny<Guid>()));
otherGrain.Returns(mockedGrain.Object);
await otherGrain.DoThing("message");

mockedGrain.Verify(x => Record.("message"), Times.Once());
```

What the preceding code does is create an instance of the mockedGrain and otherGrain. The otherGrain is set up to call the mockedGrain and pass a message. We then verify the message passed from the otherGrain to the mocked grain with the Verify method.

Additional Testing

These are some basic tests to get you moving in the right direction. There are more advanced testing scenarios where you can test using a hosted test, as what we did, or an isolated test where we don't set up the cluster. We can also test the calling to other grains along with a timer and reminder testing. This takes a decent amount of setup and dives into the cluster fixture. There is a great article written by Jorge Candeias that can be found at `https://jorgecandeias.github.io/2019/07/14/how-to-unit-test-framework-services-in-orleans/` that is a deep dive into Orleans' unit testing.

Essentially, what is done is that fakes are being created of the reminders and timers. Afterwards, they are being used to register with our testing cluster which then calls on reminders/timers for the tests. Next, various items are called within the grains to pass the tests, mocking grains, and factories to test in an isolated fashion. Finally, get responses from the grains is called on from timers, reminders, and other grains to assert their correctness.

Summary

In this chapter, we covered unit testing. The unit tests in conjunction with TestingHost allow us to test the grain logic as we would any other service. In addition, creating the ClusterFixture and ClusterCollection classes enabled us to use a single host per test run rather than reinstating per test. Unit tests are an excellent way to prove that your code works and help determine if additional features affect existing code.

Calling grains were also covered, which should be noted as a reoccurring pattern. It is an essential building block for Orleans applications, and we will see this in future development. Make sure to tuck this info into your toolkit memory.

We then ran the test. We can see that the tests, built with xUnit, run and display results. The results are shown in the test runner.

This is breaking the surface of what is available, as it can be seen in a much deeper walk-through in Jorge's article. It is up to you to decide what is the correct amount of testing that is needed to feel comfortable. It may not be required to test calls from the timers and reminders and the results of the called grains. Perhaps hosting and testing the grains themselves would suffice vs. creating an additional overhead; however, it can be accomplished.

In the next chapter, we will dive into creating a dashboard to view how our application behaves in real time.

CHAPTER 8

The Orleans Dashboard

Overview

We have set up grains and tests to validate the logic, but how do we monitor the cluster in real time? The answer is the Orleans Dashboard. This tool is not intended to replace your monitoring systems and was created to assist developers during development (Astbury, et al., 2021). It allows us to monitor a magnitude of information such as the number of requests, failures, and response time in a GUI interface. Furthermore, as you will see, it is effortless to implement. For example, when I worked in an Application Lifecycle Management (ALM) team, we had monitors added to the floor and added various health checks and a graphical interface to display the summaries. The Orleans Dashboard is not far off from the information we displayed, and it is easy to ascertain information from a glance. It is extremely helpful having this information available as you are developing.

Adding the Orlean Dashboard to Our Solution

The dashboard is a fantastic feature. I cannot praise it enough. We can view a summary of overall performance or drill down into grains, the silo, reminders, and streams. In addition, it provides a brief overview at a glance of items such as:

- Activations
- Errors
- Performance

© Thomas Nelson 2022
T. Nelson, *Introducing Microsoft Orleans*, https://doi.org/10.1007/978-1-4842-8014-0_8

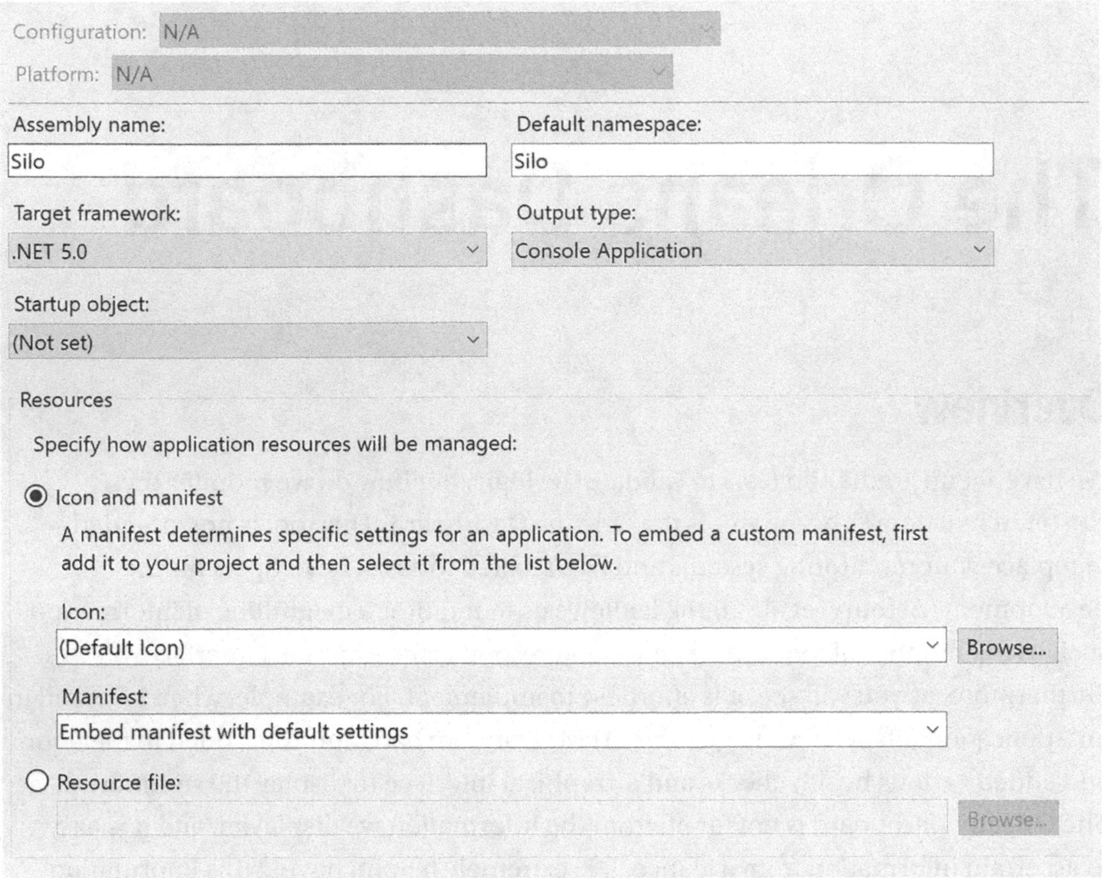

Configuration: N/A

Platform: N/A

Assembly name:

Silo

Default namespace:

Silo

Target framework:

.NET 5.0

Output type:

Console Application

Startup object:

(Not set)

Resources

Specify how application resources will be managed:

◉ Icon and manifest

A manifest determines specific settings for an application. To embed a custom manifest, first add it to your project and then select it from the list below.

Icon:

(Default Icon)   Browse...

Manifest:

Embed manifest with default settings

○ Resource file:

Browse...

Figure 8-1. *Project property. Update the target framework*

Let's begin adding the dashboard to our project. First, the dashboard requires .NET 5.0 or later. Right-click the Silo project, select Properties, and change the "Target framework" to .NET 5 or higher, as shown in Figure 8-1. Now we can add the dashboard NuGet package.

Figure 8-2. *OrleansDashboard NuGet. Selecting the latest stable version, 3.5*

Browse NuGet for the OrleansDashboard. During the writing of this book, 3.5.0 is the current stable version, as seen in Figure 8-2; however, using the latest stable version is completely acceptable. This library contains everything we need for the dashboard.

Now we need to update our code in the Silo Program.cs file. We are adding the ability to automatically detect grains of the original project and the initialization of the dashboard. We can see these in bold in the following code:

```
var builder = new SiloHostBuilder()
    .UseLocalhostClustering()
    .Configure<ClusterOptions>(options =>
    {
        options.ClusterId = "dev";
        options.ServiceId = "OrleansBasics";
    })
    .ConfigureApplicationParts(parts => parts.AddApplication
    Part(typeof(TutorialGrain).Assembly).WithReferences())
    // Enable automatic discovery of the grains of the
    original project
```

```
.ConfigureApplicationParts(parts => parts.AddFrom
ApplicationBaseDirectory())
// Initialize dashboard
.UseDashboard(options => { })
.ConfigureLogging(logging => logging.AddConsole());
```

Running the Dashboard

That's it. That's all that is needed to add a dashboard. Let's start the silo to see what was added. To see the dashboard, we need to visit the following address:

- **http://silo-address:8080**

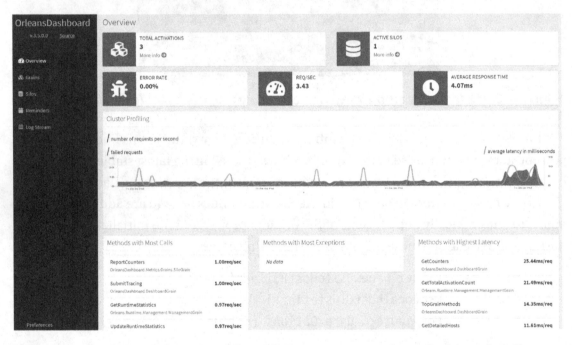

Figure 8-3. *Admin OrleansDashboard. Summary overview of grains, the silos, and overall performance*

Figure 8-3 displays the interface when visiting **<grain-address> : port 8080**. You should notice a graph that shares the ongoing number of requests and failures and latency. Above that, the error rate, activations, response time, and the number of requests are shown. Most of these samples are taken every 100 seconds and can be configured in the options that we will see later in this chapter.

Looking lower on the page, we can see the aggregated lists. Methods with Most Calls helps us determine the most common methods based on the requests per second. Methods with Most Exceptions is ordered from the highest to the lowest error rates and helps determine possible bug priorities. Latency is ordered from highest to lowest latency, so we can reevaluate our logic and possibly reduce unneeded calls.

Figure 8-4. *OrleansDashboard grains. A visual breakdown of the grains*

We selected the grains dashboard in Figure 8-4, which displays additional information about active grains. For example, the total number of grain activations, error rate, requests, and response time are available. As we scroll further down the page, tracing logistics are shared for methods.

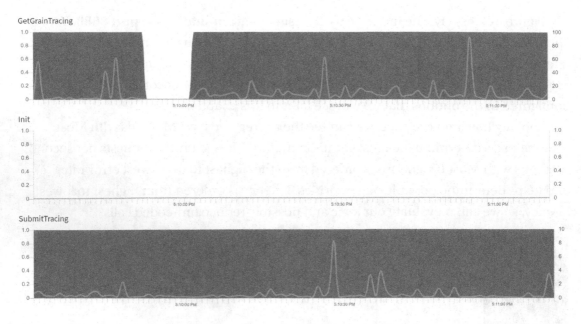

Figure 8-5. *OrleansDashboard grains continued 1. Method tracing information*

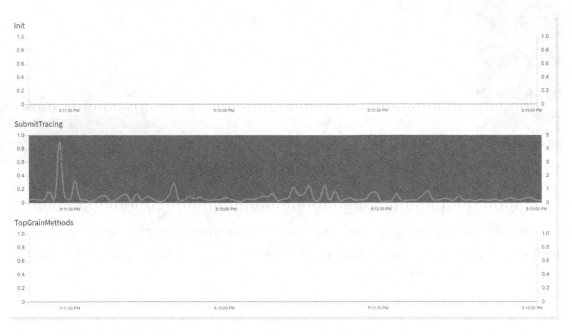

Figure 8-6. *OrleansDashboard grains continued 2. Method tracing information continued*

Individual methods are monitored. From here, we can determine how each method is performing in terms of failures and response time. This information helps us decide whether we should break up a method into smaller workloads. Methods can grow or perhaps support more functions than their intended scope. I have used various tracing tools and performance testing to "weed out" these issues. The dashboard will not remove the need for performance tests; however, it does provide decent information to analyze our performance on an individual method level, as we can see in Figures 8-5 and 8-6. Also, we can remove the system and dashboard tracing through preferences, as seen later on.

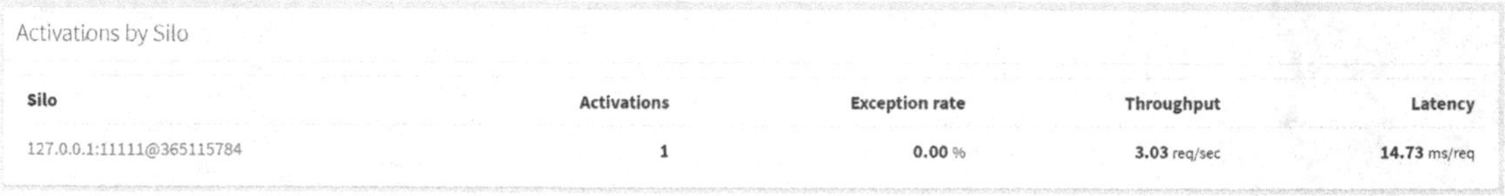

Activations by Silo				
Silo	**Activations**	**Exception rate**	**Throughput**	**Latency**
127.0.0.1:11111@365115784	1	0.00 %	3.03 req/sec	14.73 ms/req

Figure 8-7. *OrleansDashboard grains continued 3. Grain activations are displayed per silo*

At the bottom of the page, each silo is listed, as seen in Figure 8-7, along with the number of grain activations, exceptions, throughput, and latency. Each silo name is a link-to information about that individual silo, which we will see in the next section. If we were running a cluster, additional rows would show repeated information for each silo in the cluster.

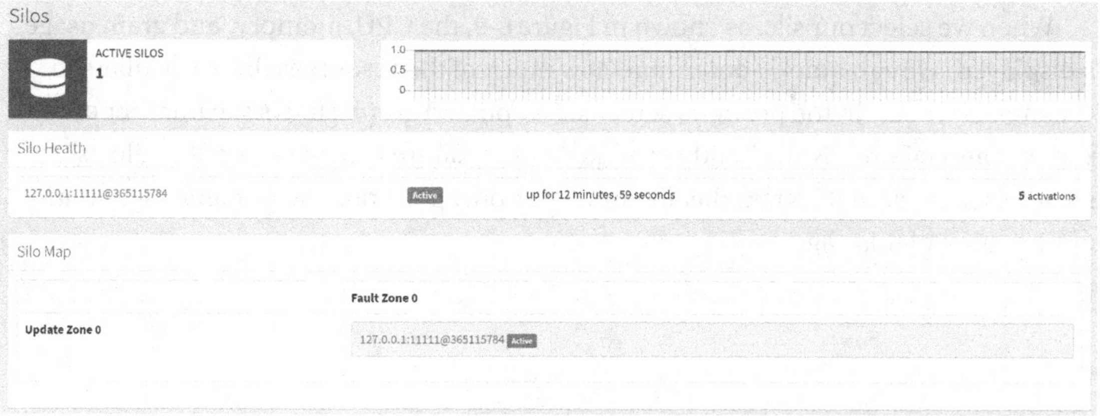

Figure 8-8. *OrleansDashboard silos. A visual breakdown of the silos*

131

If we click the Silos link in the navigation on the left, we will view the silo summary screen, as in Figure 8-8. Again, active silos and uptime are displayed. In addition, silos will be mapped to their zones. Since we are running this locally, we will see it as fault zone 0.

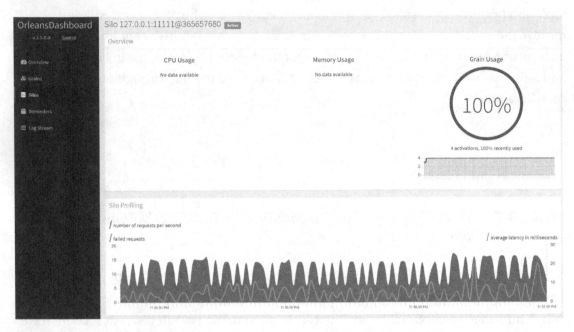

Figure 8-9. *OrleansDashboard specific silo. Detailed information about a specific silo*

When we select our silo, as shown in Figure 8-9, the CPU, memory, and grain usage is displayed. We can quickly determine how much of the resources the particular silo is using. As we saw in the previous screens, an updated graph shows the number of requests and failures. Note that these requests and failures are based on this silo as a whole, whereas, in the grain dashboard, it was on a per-grain basis. Figure 8-10 is a continuation of this page.

Silo Counters			Silo Properties	
Clients	0		Host name	DESKTOP-V6L4LPE
Messages recieved	0		Role name	Silo
Messages sent	0		Silo name	Silo_a9a2d
Receive queue	0		Proxy port	30000
Request queue	0		Update zone	0
Send queue	0		Fault zone	0
View all counters				

Activations by Type		Activations ↓	Exception rate	Throughput	Latency
SiloGrain	Dashboard Grain	1	0.00 %	1.12 req/sec	0.09 ms/req
DashboardRemindersGrain	Dashboard Grain	1	0.00 %	0.00 req/sec	0 ms/req
DashboardGrain	Dashboard Grain	1	0.00 %	1.24 req/sec	4.57 ms/req
ManagementGrain	System Grain	1	0.00 %	1.24 req/sec	6.48 ms/req

Figure 8-10. *OrleansDashboard specific silo continued. Additional page information*

We can view and filter 25 reminders per page and view the performance. Following suit of the other dashboards, we see the number of activations. If your application is not using reminders, it is empty, as we can see in Figure 8-11.

Figure 8-11. *OrleansDashboard reminders. Displays information about reminder grains and the ability filters for specific reminders*

Figure 8-12. *OrleansDashboard log stream. A continuous stream of logs*

Clicking the Log Stream item on the left navigation pane loads the real-time logging page, as seen in Figure 8-12. We can trace messages as they happen and pause the record for readability. We can see the grain starting and end of the grain requests and custom logging we would like to see. These are based on current events. The information is not persisted through the dashboard and will need to be set up separately, such as storing it in Azure Storage.

Figure 8-13. *OrleansDashboard preferences. Choosing our settings*

The bottom of the menu has an item by the name of Preferences. Here we can remove the dashboard and system grains from counters, graphs, and tables. This allows our custom grains to take front and center. Also, the theme can be changed between light and dark. So, for example, we can see the dark theme in Figure 8-13.

Additional Options

The developers developed additional options for security and customizing where the dashboard should be displayed and how often it should update. It is simple to edit the code to add these items, as seen in the following:

```
// Define the cluster configuration
    var builder = new SiloHostBuilder()
        .UseLocalhostClustering()
        .Configure<ClusterOptions>(options =>
        {
            options.ClusterId = "dev";
            options.ServiceId = "OrleansBasics";
        })
                        .ConfigureApplicationParts(parts => parts.
                        AddApplicationPart(typeof(TutorialGrain).
                        Assembly).WithReferences())
    // Enable automatic discovery of the grains of the
        original project
.ConfigureApplicationParts(parts => parts.
AddFromApplicationBaseDirectory())
    // Initialize dashboard
    .UseDashboard(options => {
        // Dashboard Access - basic authentication
        options.Username = "USERNAME";
        options.Password = "PASSWORD";
        // Binding to webserver; * is default
        options.Host = "*";
        // Set port number
        options.Port = 8080;
        // Dashboard hosts its own http server; default is true
        options.HostSelf = true;
        // Intervals, in milliseconds, between sampling
        options.CounterUpdateIntervalMs = 1000;
    })
```

Sign in to access this site

Authorization required by http://127.0.0.1:8080

Username

Password

Sign in   Cancel

Figure 8-14. *Basic authentication. A sign-in dialog box*

After updating the code, run a new instance of the silo, and then navigate your browser to 127.0.0.1:8080, or whatever port you chose. For example, if you added the username and password options, you would be prompted to enter the credentials in Figure 8-14 and click Sign in. Afterward, you will be taken to the admin dashboard we saw in Figure 8-3.

Expanding the Dashboard

If the UI doesn't contain everything that is needed, we can add to it. It is written in react.js. Node.js and npm are required for the development. The UI components and dependencies are stored within the index.min.js file.

An HTTP API is available for external tools to consume that supports:

- DashboardCounters

  - A summary of cluster metrics, which includes a summary and a count of active silos and grains

- Historical stats

  - Latest 100 samples of the silo's statistics

- Silo properties

  - Properties of a specific silo

- Grain stats

  - Grain method profiling counter aggregated across all of the silos within the past 100 seconds

- Cluster stats

  - Aggregated grain method profiling counters collected from the entire cluster in the past 100 seconds

- Silo stats

  - Aggregated grain methods profiling counters from a specific silo from the past 100 seconds

- Top grain methods

  - The five top grain methods based on requests per second, error rate, and latency

- Reminders

  - A count of the total number of reminders and a page containing up to 25 reminders

- Trace

  - Streams a trace log

Further information can be found here: https://github.com/OrleansContrib/OrleansDashboard.

The dashboard repository contains several applications that you can run to see how they are perceived in the dashboard. They can be found here: https://github.com/OrleansContrib/OrleansDashboard/tree/master/Tests/TestHosts.

Summary

In this chapter, we learned about the Orleans Dashboard and how much information we can gather at a glance. For example, we can see grain activations, latency, average response time, and error percentage and expand the interface if required. I am excited about this feature, coming from an ALM/DecSecOps mindset, since it neatly displays much information. Please recall that it was created as a developer support tool and is not built for production use.

On the admin page, silo and grain activations are seen, along with the number of requests per second, failed requests, and the average latency. In addition, we can drill into specific information about specific grains and silos. We can also see real-time tracing on the dashboard and pause the logs to review particular items.

We can change the skin of the dashboard to dark mode if we are inclined to do so. The system and dashboard grains can be removed from the graphs. So we can use the real estate for the custom grains that we created.

We are able to extend the dashboard through several means. First, we can add options to add security, hosting locations, and updating intervals. Second, we can further develop the UI by updating the index.min.js file. Finally, we can also consume the information for our personal use and persist it if needed. HTTP API endpoints are available to consume the same information that is being displayed on the dashboard for your project's needs, such as for historical analysis.

The dashboard is easy to implement into our project, as we learned by adding the library and dependency injection. It provides a significant amount of information with little effort. It is an easy win for monitoring and visual support, and I believe it should be implemented on most, if not all, occasions.

## CHAPTER 9

Deployment

This chapter will demonstrate how to move our application from our local machine to a remote host. Deployment encompasses more than building and driving an application from points A to B. We need to determine if items are deployable based on compatibility and hosting support. Also, a pipeline will be used for deployment when needed, which encompasses Continuous Integration (CI) and Continuous Delivery/Deployment (CD). These are commonly used terms in DevOps and are generally referred to as CI/CD. Several aspects extend beyond this book's reach, such as in-depth automated testing and multiple-environment setup. However, we will briefly cover them to provide an understanding for future reference.

We will be using a deployment script to remove the complex infrastructure setup on the DevOps side. Otherwise, we will deter from the Orleans topic and spend a significant amount of time on a complex pipeline. The scripts will create an Azure environment for the deployment process. We will also deploy our local machine's initial deployment through the scripts. After the initial deployment, commits will trigger the building of the application and the deployment to the AKS cluster.

Compatible Grains

Compatible grains are defined as, "When an existing grain activation is about to process a request, the runtime will check if the version in the request and the actual version of the grain are compatible (Microsoft, n.d.)." allow backward compatibility. Backward compatibility means that if there are two or more versions of an interface, the runtime will determine if it can process the request normally or will it need to spin up another grain from the compatible interface. To be compatible:

- Grain interfaces remain unchanged.

- Inherited signatures remain unchanged.

- Methods are not removed from interfaces.

T. Nelson, *Introducing Microsoft Orleans*, https://doi.org/10.1007/978-1-4842-8014-0_9

The method signature must remain unchanged to be compatible, such as the intake and the response. In addition, the accessibility cannot be changed. For example, a public method cannot be made private and expected to be compatible. There are also *fully compatible grains* when we meet backward compatible grain requirements and didn't add public methods. In the following we can see a breakdown of a method signature:

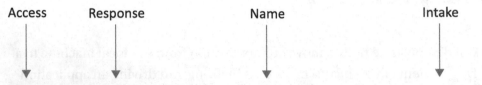

public Task<string> GetLatest10UserNames(int id, string guid)

Figure 9-1. *Method signature. The access allows the method to be seen by a specific scope, and the response is the return type – the method name, which should be written to explain the scope and action of the method. Finally, the intake consists of the variables, if any, that are required to process the request*

As displayed in Figure 9-1, Access, Response, Name, and Intake items cannot be modified to be backward compatible. A runtime error may occur if the public access is set to private. However, we can always add additional methods to the grain.

According to the Orleans Contribution (Astbury, et al., n.d.) repo, the production performance expectations with Microsoft Azure Virtual Machine consist of:

- 8 CPU cores
- 14 gigabytes of RAM
- 1 silo per VM

Results of the tests (Astbury, et al., n.d.):

- 1,000 maximum requests per grain per second.
- 10,000 requests per second.
- 100,000 grains can be active in the silo.

Our deployment will not use the same-size VM (s) due to cost. You are welcome to make the change as needed, but we are scoping this to simply deploy and not worry as much about performance. Production use costs are another venture beyond this book.

Database Handling (Deployment)

Scripts are provided to start the persistence setup. Orleans' documentation sets up databases by sharing templates for SQL Server, MySQL, MariaDB, PostgreSQL, and Oracle. The scripts set up the base tables for Orleans, clusters, persistence, and reminders. Templates that can be used for on-premise or remote setup can be found here: `https://dotnet.github.io/orleans/docs/host/configuration_guide/adonet_configuration.html`. We would have to set up the database before we run these scripts to set up the tables. It is a simple process, although we must be aware of the limited access users will have when we set up higher-level environments, which means either Database Administrators (DBAs) or deployment scripts may be needed for setup.

We have previously learned that each grain has the ability to connect to a database. However, using the persistent data object is easier to gather the information while the grain is being activated. It was developed – as an optional use – to easily connect to the database. It allows the database call to be made simultaneously as the grain is instantiated. A typical DB call is entirely acceptable if data is needed after the grain has been initiated. This reduced the effort of DB implementation and shaves off compute time.

Also, grain persistence saves the grains from the last time they were active or based on the previous active state. This means that whatever event last occurred, the grains will reactivate as if they were always running. Several databases are deemed, by Microsoft, to officially support the storage, and additional can be found on the community contribution GitHub site. The officially supported databases are (Microsoft, n.d.):

- *Azure Storage* – An inexpensive and scalable storage

- *Amazon DynamoDB* – NoSQL database

- *SQL Server* – SQL Server database

Cluster Management

We touched on cluster management in Chapter 3. We learned how cluster health is monitored and determined through a heartbeat regarding deployment. Ultimately, the clusters self-policing or can be see as a neighborhood watch. A silo signs itself into the MembershipTable when it joins the cluster. The silos will ping one another to determine health. For instance, silos will ping one another, and if it is not getting a response, then it is flagged as a possible failure. If the flagged silo continues with failed responses, then the suspicious cluster is considered dead, and communication is no longer sent to that silo. There will be health checks to determine if the cluster returns and resumes communications.

The following are MembershipTable-compatible storage options (Microsoft, n.d.):

- *Azure Table Storage* – NoSQL DB

- *SQL Server* – SQL Server database

- *Apache ZooKeeper* – Synchronized distributed systems (Kafka)

- *Consul IO* – Multi-environment service orchestration

- *AWS DynamoDB* – NoSQL database

- *In-Memory* – Local temporary storage

CI/CD Overview

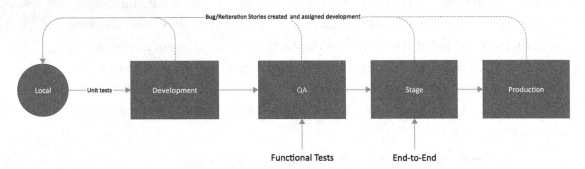

Figure 9-2. *CI/CD basic pipeline. This figure depicts the pathway of deployment to multiple environments. The Integration environment was left out as it's not always used. It fits between Development and Quality Assurance (QA)*

When creating a pipeline, as seen in Figure 9-2, it begins on a local development machine. It is good to implement Test Driven Development (TDD), where we write unit tests as we write the functions. It allows developers to test specific code pieces and determine if future additions have broken previous logic. Unit tests should be set to be required to pass before being deployed to the Development environment. Each environment is set to test different aspects of the application, and the number of environments is dependent on the organization's need. As shown

- The Development environment are for initial deployments, which is one step about running it on your local machine. This should happen after a code review and gatekeeper/reviewer approvess the commit which allows it to complete. After that, the Dev environment is used to determine that applications are deploying successfully and for basic testing.

- The Initial environment (Int) is used to test how the application integrates/communicates with other applications.

- The QA environment is reserved for functional testing of the business logic traditionally performed by QA personnel by submitting requests and determining if the response matches the expected reply.

- The Stage environment should be a mirror image, other than data, of the production environment. Since this environment mimics prod, integration and end-to-end testing should be performed as a final step before production deployment.

- The Production environment should always be hosted on machines, networks, and data. This environment directly serves the client.

Environments can be physical or logical. Physical environments place the applications on separate servers. This can be expensive. Logical separation can be done by physically separating the production environment from lower environments (Dev, Int, QA, and Stage) on different machines. Of course these can be expanded per budget and requirements, but the concept is isolate the production server. Logically environments are separated by code or software, such as including feature flagging, which allows you to turn on and off features in the code based on the environment you are emulating. It is a modular approach that helps specific items "flip" as needed. It can be reversed without redeploying the code based on its implementation.

If you would like to expand your DevOps knowledge, here are some wonderful sites to get started:

- Introduction to DevOps

  - `https://azure.microsoft.com/en-us/overview/what-is-devops`

  - This is a great starting point to learn DevOps. It will walk you through processes, tools, and diagrams.

- Quick reference

  - https://docs.microsoft.com/en-us/devops

  - This site is packed with information to help you implement and understand DevOps. It is a great future reference site.

- LaunchDarkly

  - https://launchdarkly.com

  - LaunchDarkly is software that is built upon feature flagging. The implementation is relatively easy and is outstanding for managing feature flags.

Multiple-environment setups can be challenging to maintain, especially with multiple people pushing code. A way to maintain work with features and activity is typically associated with scrum where it associates work items with resources. These work items are bite-size pieces of work completed and pushed into the environments after proper gate control. When an issue is found, it can be associated with the original work item to be corrected.

Depending on the bug found, it might need to be fixed immediately or pushed for a later release. If you choose to implement feature flags, this is easily pushed on its own when it's been completed. However, if you decide to push a release as a group, additional overhead is needed to align completion times and thoroughness.

Additional deployment strategies can help alleviate these issues. This allows us to manipulate where the traffic flows for varying deployment types. These lower the blast radius for when problems occur.Deployment Strategies:

- *Canary* – Deployments are done in small increments such as 3% that can grow to 100% in production. This allows a set number of real users to be testers.

- *Blue Green* – This deployment essentially flips the Stage and Production environments by switching traffic with a load balancer. It have a quick failover time when needed by flipping the environments again.

- *A/B Testing* – We release different versions of the same service to the environment. This allows us to explore varying features of the service to see which works the best with the users.

The preceding deployment types were mentioned to provide options. DevOps is a vast area and is constantly innovating. We will not pursue any of these in this chapter; however, I wanted to share some concepts for future deployments. Another tool for the toolbelt.

Common Deployment Scenarios

Use an Azure table to cluster membership when services are deployed to Azure. Azure tables are easily set up, inexpensive, highly available, and scalable. The pairing creates the ability to quickly set up the application with low overhead and easy maintainability.

SQL Server is another dependable option to use instead of Azure tables. SQL can be hosted in multiple clouds, which creates a cloud-agnostic approach. SQL Server or Postgres can be used but can be expensive. SQLite is another option embedded in your application and doesn't require additional servers.

However, if you are concerned about testing the cluster on a remote machine, the MembershipTableGrain can be used instead (Microsoft, n.d.). It is not consistent, but you will pass transactions on a remote device. *MembershipTableGrains were not made to be used this way for production use.*

Setting Up the Azure Environment

The following are prerequisites for following this walk-through:

- *A Personal Azure Subscription* – If you do not have an existing Azure subscription, Microsoft generally provides new subscribers with 12 months of limited free services and a $200 credit to explore Azure for 30 days. Please visit `https://azure.microsoft.com` for more information. Students can get a $100 credit on Azure through this link `https://azure.microsoft.com/en-us/free/students/`.

- *A Personal GitHub Account That Includes Creating Actions for Your Code Repositories* – Please visit `https://github.com` for more information. If you are a student, check out the Student Developer Pack by visiting `https://education.github.com/pack`.

- *Azure CLI* – Azure CLI is a platform-agnostic command-line interface tool that can run in the Windows command line, Linux terminals, PowerShell/PowerShell core, and Linux/Unix-based shell scripts. For installation instructions, please visit `https://docs.microsoft.com/en-us/cli/azure/install-azure-cli`.

One last disclaimer before diving into the walk-through: You will be charged for the computing and storage costs for some of the resources created in the following. Therefore, it is recommended that once you are satisfied with your deployment, you destroy the resource group and all resources contained within to prevent getting an unexpected bill.

Walk-Through to Create a CI/CD Pipeline

In Chapter 3, we talked about the local vs. production deployments before diving into the walk-through. To streamline the process and be palatable, we will release without breaking the items into separate items such as a NuGet feed. Otherwise, we will be travelling well beyond the scope of this book. GitHub can publish the libraries as NuGet packages by using this action: `https://github.com/marketplace/actions/publish-nuget`. This NuGet action will package the library(s) and deploy it to `https://api.nuget.org`.

Initial Setup

To walk us through the setup of a pipeline without making it overly complex, we create and run local scripts that connect to Azure that provides the infrastructure and does the initial deployment. Otherwise, we need to develop additional authentication for the deployment that allows resource allocation. This book is not aimed at intermediate or advanced DevOps, and it would deter Orleans' deployment learnings. Therefore, we will use the following scrips that build the initial resource structure. Then, we will create a CI/CD pipeline that deploys the latest code triggered upon a commit.

These documents were taken from `https://github.com/ReubenBond/hanbaobao-web`, which is HanBaoBao – Orleans's sample application by Reuben Bond. They can be found in the following:

- *provision.ps1* – Create items such as the resource group, AKS cluster, and service principles.

  - `https://github.com/ReubenBond/hanbaobao-web/blob/main/provision.ps1`

- *Dockerfile* – We will create this within Visual Studio.

  - `https://github.com/ReubenBond/hanbaobao-web/blob/main/Dockerfile`

- *deployment.yaml* – Detailed information to implement resources.

  - `https://github.com/ReubenBond/hanbaobao-web/blob/main/deployment.yaml`

- *deploy.ps1* – Deploys the docker image to AKS.

  - `https://github.com/ReubenBond/hanbaobao-web/blob/main/deploy.ps1`

Creating Resources with Azure CLI

The following scripts will contain all the commands we need to create all required Azure resources, which can be executed line by line by copying and pasting them into your preferred terminal. A comment above the execution line will inform you what the script creates. Please see the links at the end of the chapter to learn more about these resources and possible configurations.

We need to start housecleaning to set up our resources and release files. First, we add a few folders to the repo to add our CI/CD scripts and compartmentalize supporting scripts. The items are

- .github/workflows

  - This folder is recognized by GitHub and will be checked for deployment scripts.

  - Here we will add

    - Continous-delivery.yaml

      - This is the script that deploys our work to AKS.

- Continous-integration.yaml

    - This is the script that builds our code and runs the unit tests.

- _create-azure-resources

    - This folder houses the scripts that create the resources in Azure. We have them written in Bash and PowerShell.

        - Bash_resource_provision.sh

        - Pwsh_resource_provision.ps1

- _manifests

    - This folder contains detailed information about our deployment.

        - Deployment.yaml

- <root directory>

    - This is the base folder that contains all the files in the repo.

        - Dockerfile

            - Commands to build a docker image

Provisioning Scripts

Location: /_create-azure-resources

The provisioning scripts create the same resources. You are welcome to use the Bash or the PowerShell script. I chose PowerShell since it can be troubleshot with PowerShell ISE.

PowerShell can be installed on multiple operating system types: Windows, macOS, and Linux. More information can be found here: `https://docs.microsoft.com/en-us/powershell/scripting/install/installing-powershell?msclkid=460a2ad5a1d111ec84eb7d5035aaaf73&view=powershell-7.2`.

Make sure you provision the resources before deployment. This can be done in the Azure Portal command line or PowerShell or by using the command line or PowerShell on your local machine.

Azure CLI can be installed from here: https://docs.microsoft.com/en-us/cli/azure/install-azure-cli-windows?tabs=azure-cli. There is a macOS and Linux version as well.

The Azure PowerShell module can be added from here: https://docs.microsoft.com/en-us/powershell/azure/install-az-ps?msclkid=1a38dbffa30211ec96b5eb5d8b260406&view=azps-7.3.0.

Pwsh_resource_provision.ps1 Code (PowerShell)

```
# Powershell script

# Instructions
# The azure command line tool, az cli does not have great blocking for
processes
# In order to make sure things happen in the correct order, we recommend
executing
# each command separately in your IDE. In VS Code, you can highlight
code and use
# F8 to execute the highlighted code
# Set your resource name variables here. The following are for example purposes
$resourceGroup = "orleansbasics"
$location = "eastus"
$storageAccount = "orleansbasics1"
$clusterName = "orleansbasics"
$containerRegistry = "orleansbasicsacr1"

# Opens a browser tab to log in to Azure
az login
# Create a resource group
az group create --name $resourceGroup --location $location
# Create an Azure storage account
az storage account create --location $location --name
$storageAccount --resource-group $resourceGroup --kind "StorageV2" --sku
"Standard_LRS"

# If you haven't already, install the Kubernetes CLI
az aks install-cli
```

```
# Create an Azure Container Registry account and login to it
az acr create --name $containerRegistry --resource-group
$resourceGroup --sku basic
$acrId = $(az acr show --name $containerRegistry --query id --output tsv)
# Create an AKS cluster. This can take a few minutes
az aks create --resource-group $resourceGroup --name $clusterName --node-
count 1 --generate-ssh-keys --attach-acr $acrId
# Authenticate the Kubernetes CLI
az aks get-credentials --resource-group $resourceGroup --name $clusterName
# Configure the storage account that the application is going to use by
adding a new secret to Kubernetes
kubectl create secret generic az-storage-acct --from-literal=key=$(az
storage account show-connection-string --name $storageAccount --resource-
group $resourceGroup --output tsv)
```

Bash_resource_provision.sh Code (Command Line)

```
#!/bin/bash
# Instructions
# The azure command line tool, az cli does not have great blocking for
processes
# In order to make sure things happen in the correct order, we recommend
executing
# each command separately in your IDE. In VS Code, you can highlight
code and use
# F8 to execute the highlighted code
# Set your resource name variables here. The following are for example
purposes
resourceGroup="orleansbasics"
location="eastus"
storageAccount="orleansbasics1"
clusterName="orleansbasics"
containerRegistry="orleansbasicsacr"
# Opens a browser tab to log in to Azure
az login
# Create a resource group
```

```
az group create --name $resourceGroup --location $location
# Create an Azure storage account
az storage account create --location $location --name
$storageAccount --resource-group $resourceGroup --kind "StorageV2" --sku
"Standard_LRS"
# Create an Azure Container Registry account and login to it
az acr create --name $containerRegistry --resource-group
$resourceGroup --sku basic
acrId=$(az acr show --name $containerRegistry --query id --output tsv)
# If you haven't already, install the Kubernetes CLI
az aks install-cli
# Create an AKS cluster. This can take a few minutes
az aks create --resource-group $resourceGroup --name $clusterName --node-
count 1 --generate-ssh-keys --attach-acr $acrId

# Authenticate the Kubernetes CLI
az aks get-credentials --resource-group $resourceGroup --name $clusterName
# Configure the storage account that the application is going to use by
adding a new secret to Kubernetes
kubectl create secret generic az-storage-acct --from-literal=key=$(az
storage account show-connection-string --name $storageAccount --resource-
group $resourceGroup --output tsv)
```

Provision Script Summary

The provisioning file is used to sign in to Azure. The primary components are added:

- Connecting account to Azure

- Creating a resource group

  - A resource group is a logical grouping of items.

  - You can delete all of the things within the resource group by deleting the resource group.

- Creating an AKS cluster

- Installing AKS CLI if it isn't already installed

- Creating storage account

Deployment Files

Dockerfile

We start by making the Dockerfile. The easiest way to create this file is by opening the Introduction solution. Then, Visual Studio will create the file for us.

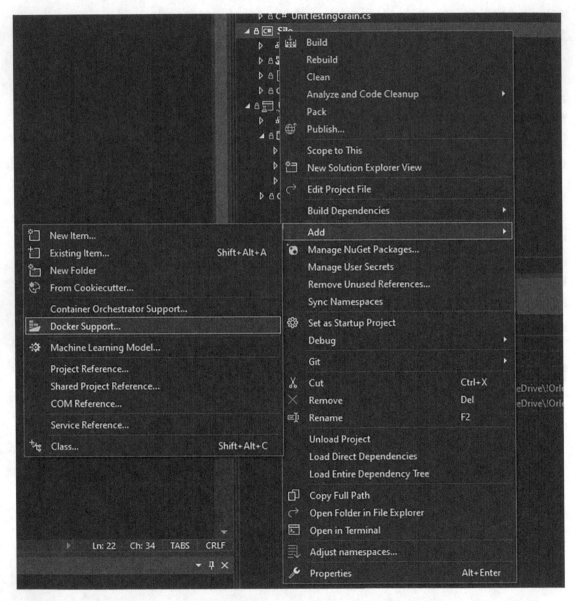

Figure 9-3. *Visual Studio creates the Dockerfile. It is an automated feature that makes creating docker images simplistic.*

Figure 9-3 shows us how to create the Dockerfile. Right-click the Silo project and select Add. You will see the Docker Support option. Select it to create the file.

Dockerfile Code

```
Location: root
#See https://aka.ms/containerfastmode understand how Visual Studio uses
this Dockerfile to build your images for faster debugging.
FROM mcr.microsoft.com/dotnet/runtime:3.1 AS base
WORKDIR /app
FROM mcr.microsoft.com/dotnet/sdk:3.1 AS build
WORKDIR /src
COPY ["Silo/Silo.csproj", "Silo/"]
COPY ["GrainInterfaces/GrainInterfaces.csproj", "GrainInterfaces/"]
COPY ["Grains/Grains.csproj", "Grains/"]
RUN dotnet restore "Silo/Silo.csproj"
COPY . .
WORKDIR "/src/Silo"
RUN dotnet build "Silo.csproj" -c Release -o /app/build
FROM build AS publish
RUN dotnet publish "Silo.csproj" -c Release -o /app/publish
FROM base AS final
WORKDIR /app
COPY --from=publish /app/publish .
ENTRYPOINT ["dotnet", "Silo.dll"]
```

Dockerfile Summary

The Dockerfile is used to create the image. The Dockerfile generates the silo image that we deploy and host in AKS. It copies the necessary files, builds them, and then publishes the built application.

Deployment.yaml

Location: /_manifests

The deployment script is used to set up the specifics of our resources. We pull the image and host it. We use our service principle and secrets to set up and deploy the app. We also set up a load balancer for our application to make it available for consumption from outside of AKS.

Deployment.yaml Code

```yaml
# In order to be able to access the service from outside the cluster, we
will need to add a Service object of type LoadBalancer
apiVersion: v1
kind: Service
metadata:
  name: orleansbasics
spec:
  type: LoadBalancer
  ports:
  - port: 80
  selector:
    app: orleansbasics
---
# For RBAC-enabled clusters, the Kubernetes service account for the pods
may also need to be granted the required access:
kind: Role
apiVersion: rbac.authorization.k8s.io/v1
metadata:
  name: pod-reader
rules:
- apiGroups: [ "" ]
  resources: ["pods"]
  verbs: ["get", "watch", "list"]
---
kind: RoleBinding
```

```yaml
apiVersion: rbac.authorization.k8s.io/v1
metadata:
  name: pod-reader-binding
subjects:
- kind: ServiceAccount
  name: default
  apiGroup: "
roleRef:
  kind: Role
  name: pod-reader
  apiGroup: "
---
apiVersion: apps/v1
kind: Deployment
metadata:
  name: orleansbasics
  labels:
    app: orleansbasics
spec:
  selector:
    matchLabels:
      app: orleansbasics
  replicas: 3
  template:
    metadata:
      labels:
        app: orleansbasics
        # The serviceId label is used to identify the service to Orleans
        orleans/serviceId: orleansbasics
        # The clusterId label is used to identify an instance of a cluster
        to Orleans.
        # Typically, this will be the same value as serviceId or any
        fixed value.
        # In cases where you are not using rolling deployments (for
        example, blue/green deployments),
```

```
      # this value can allow for distinct clusters which do not
      communicate directly with each other, but which still share the
      same storage and other resources.
      orleans/clusterId: dev
spec:
  containers:
    - name: main
      image: orleansbasicsacr1.azurecr.io/orleansbasics
      imagePullPolicy: Always
      ports:
      # Define the ports which Orleans uses
      - containerPort: 11111
      - containerPort: 30000
      # Define the ASP.NET Core ports
      - containerPort: 80
      - containerPort: 443
      env:

      # The Azure Storage connection string for clustering is injected
      as an environment variable
      # It must be created separately using a command such as:
      # > kubectl create secret generic az-storage-acct --from-
      file=key=./az-storage-acct.txt
      - name: STORAGE_CONNECTION_STRING
        valueFrom:
          secretKeyRef:
            name: az-storage-acct
            key: key
      # Configure settings to let Orleans know which cluster it belongs
      to and which pod it is running in
      - name: ORLEANS_SERVICE_ID
        valueFrom:
          fieldRef:
            fieldPath: metadata.labels['orleans/serviceId']
      - name: ORLEANS_CLUSTER_ID
```

```
        valueFrom:
          fieldRef:
            fieldPath: metadata.labels['orleans/clusterId']
    - name: POD_NAMESPACE
      valueFrom:
        fieldRef:
          fieldPath: metadata.namespace
    - name: POD_NAME
      valueFrom:
        fieldRef:
          fieldPath: metadata.name
    - name: POD_IP
      valueFrom:
        fieldRef:
          fieldPath: status.podIP
    - name: DOTNET_SHUTDOWNTIMEOUTSECONDS
      value: "120"
terminationGracePeriodSeconds: 180
```

Deployment.yaml File Summary

This file associates several items:

- The Orleans ClusterId and ServiceId.

  - This is used to uniquely identify the Orleans silo.

- Ports are assigned to allow communication between silos and clusters.

  - Ports 11111 and 30000 are default values for Orleans.

  - Ports 80 and 443 are for HTTP and HTTPS/SSL.

- Azure storage account setup.

- Orleans is associated with the cluster and pods.

- Kubernetes setup.

- DOTNET_SHUTDOWNTIMEOUTSECONDS

    - Graceful shutdown time

- terminationGracePeriodSeconds

    - Additional time to shut down. This is used if it may take longer than the graceful shutdown at times.

- minReadySeconds

    - Minimum time for the container to be considered available for use

- rollingUpdate

    - The version is updated by the maxSurge value in each iteration until all services have been updated.

- Load balancer is set up for external access.

- Rolebinding grants access.

Continuous Integration and Continuous Delivery Pipeline Creation

The CI/CD script is triggered anytime we approve for code added to the main branch. In addition, GitHub monitors the folder structure of .github/workflows. Then, it will check for the integration and delivery steps of the pipeline named

- Continuous-integration.yaml

- Continuous-delivery.yaml

    - Deployment.yaml is *not* added here since it is a file being called by the pipeline. It illustrates the ability to modulate our code.

The integration script will be run first to build and test our artifact. It depends on what the developer decides on this section. Testing is optional but highly recommended. Additional items such as web hooks can be added to start other processes or pass information for reporting purposes.

If the integration script completes successfully, then the delivery script will run. This is used to take the asset/image and place it on the hosted server. In our case, the image is placed in the Azure Container Registry and then pushed to AKS. Once this script is successfully run, the application will be in production and available to the users.

Continuous-Integration.yaml

Location: /.github/workflows

The continuous script, as stated previously, is used to build our application. We can also run tests to validate if it is ready to be deployed to the environment. In our script, we allow the script to stop the process if the tests fail.

Continuous-Integration.yaml Code

```
###################################################################
# These workflows are for demonstrations purposes only and should not be
used in production #
###################################################################
# To learn more about GitHub Actions, please see the official
documentation:                  #
# - https://docs.github.com/en/actions/learn-github-actions/understanding-
github-actions     #
#
# To learn more about the actions used, please refer to the GitHub
marketplace:
#
# - https://github.com/marketplace
###################################################################
name: Build - Continuous Integration
# The 'on' code block below demonstrates that if branch protections are
enabled, that
# continuous integration (CI), or build, workflows will execute anytime
changes are pushed
```

```yaml
# to a branch that is not main/master, and when a PR to main/master
is created
on:
  pull_request:
    branches:
      - 'master'
  push:
    branches-ignore:
      - '!master'
jobs:
  build:
    runs-on: ubuntu-latest

    steps:
    # Checkouts the associated repository for this workflow
    - uses: actions/checkout@v2
    # Ensures we have the proper dotnet SDK installed for downstream tasks
    - name: Setup .NET Core SDK
      uses: actions/setup-dotnet@v2.0.0
      with:
        # Optional SDK version(s) to use. If not provided, will install
        global.json version when available. Examples: 2.2.104, 3.1, 3.1.x

        dotnet-version: 3.1.x
    # dotnet restore pulls in any NuGet packages required by a solution
    - name: Install dependencies
      run: dotnet restore
    # Since this is the continuous integration (CI) step, we only need to
    build our application. We will
    # execute a similar step on the release pipeline, but instead of build,
    we will use publish
    - name: Build
      run: dotnet build --configuration Release --no-restore
    # This command will execute a solution's unit tests and output the
    resulting logs to the the
    # specified results directory, "TestResults"
```

```
- name: Test
  run: dotnet test --no-restore --verbosity normal --logger
  trx --results-directory "TestResults"
# While not required, it is always a good practice to publish artifacts
veifying the state of this commit
- name: Upload dotnet test results
  uses: actions/upload-artifact@v3
  # The always() condition below will ensure that the test results are
  published even if there are test failures
  if: ${{ always() }}
  with:
    name: test-results
    path: TestResults
# Typically enterprise applications would have other steps in a
continuous integration process.
# The idea is that we want to use CI as a first opportunity to "shift
left" on any potential
# issues. Steps may include items such as:
# - security/vulnerability scans
# - code quality scans
# - add other stuff here... lol
```

Continuous-Integration.yaml Summary

This script runs every time code is merged to master. It will build an artifact and test it. If there is an error with the build or test results do not pass, the process is halted.

Continuous-delivery.yaml

Location: /.github/workflows

The delivery script, as stated previously, is used to deploy our application. It adds the image to the Azure Container Registry (ACR) and adds the image to the pod(s) in the AKS cluster. Also, it will set up a load balancer so applications that are external to the cluster can communicate with our application. Finally, if there is an error with the deployment, it will halt.

Continuous-delivery.yaml Code

```
#############################################################################
# These workflows are for demonstrations purposes only and should not be
used in production #
#############################################################################
# To learn more about GitHub Actions, please see the official
documentation:               #
# - https://docs.github.com/en/actions/learn-github-actions/understanding-
github-actions     #
#                         #
# To learn more about the actions used, please refer to the GitHub
marketplace:                 #
# - https://github.com/
marketplace                                                         #
#############################################################################
name: Deploy - Continous Delivery
# The 'on' code block below demonstrates that if branch protections are
enabled, that
# the only time a continuous delivery (CD) workflow will execute is when a
pull request
# is merged into the main branch
on:
  push:
    branches:
      - 'master'


# The 'env' block is used for declaring environment variables that will be
used in our
# workflow. These variables can be recalled by using the expressions syntax
'${{ <expression. }}'
# For more information on expressions and retrieving environment variables
and secrets, see
# https://docs.github.com/en/actions/learn-github-actions/expressions
```

```
env:
  # set this to the name of your container registry
  AZURE_CONTAINER_REGISTRY: orleansbasicsacr1
  # set this to your project's name
  PROJECT_NAME: orleansbasics
  # set this to the resource group containing your AKS cluster
  RESOURCE_GROUP: orleansbasics
  # set this to the name of your AKS cluster
  CLUSTER_NAME: orleansbasics
  # set this to the name pf your container registry url
  REGISTRY_URL: orleansbasicsacr1.azurecr.io
  # set this to the path to your helm file
  MANIFEST_PATH: _manifests/deployment.yaml
jobs:
  docker-build-and-deploy:
    # Defines the runner we want to use for executing this workflow.
    # More about choosing a runner: https://docs.github.com/en/actions/
    using-jobs/choosing-the-runner-for-a-job
    runs-on: ubuntu-latest
    steps:
    # Checkouts the associated repository for this workflow
    - uses: actions/checkout@master
    # Login to Azure using the official action
    - name: Azure Login
      uses: azure/login@v1
      with:
        creds: ${{ secrets.AZURE_CREDENTIALS }}
    # Sets default azure container registry using the AZURE_CONTAINER_
    REGISTRY environment variable
    # then builds the container image on the ACR. We could also build the
    image using docker tasks,
    # or a docker cli script
    - name: Build image on ACR
      uses: azure/CLI@v1
      with:
        azcliversion: 2.30.0
```

```
      inlineScript: |
        az configure --defaults acr=${{ env.AZURE_CONTAINER_REGISTRY }}
        az acr build -t ${{ env.REGISTRY_URL }}/${{ env.PROJECT_NAME
          }}:latest .
        # Makes sure we have kubectl (kubernetes cli tool) installed on the
        runner. It should be here, but
# better safe than sorry...

- name: Setup Kubectl
  uses: azure/setup-kubectl@v2.0
# Pulls the kubeconfig file and sets it as the default context for
executing kubectl commands against
- name: Gets K8s context
  uses: azure/aks-set-context@v1
  with:
      creds: ${{ secrets.AZURE_CREDENTIALS }}
      resource-group: ${{ env.RESOURCE_GROUP }}
      cluster-name: ${{ env.CLUSTER_NAME }}
# Deploy our application using the manifest file found at the path
defined in the MANIFEST_PATH
# environment variable
- name: Deploy our Orleans application!
  uses: Azure/k8s-deploy@v1.4
  with:
    manifests: ${{ env.MANIFEST_PATH }}
```

Continuous-delivery.yaml Summary

This script runs every time code is merged to master and the integration is completed successfully. We select the provisioned resources we want to use and pass credentials along with specifics based on the deployment.yaml file. It takes the artifact and places the image in the container registry. The image is then placed and started in a pod in our AKS cluster. A load balancer was implemented to allow access from applications that are external to the cluster.

If you would like to learn more about AKS, please follow this link: https://docs. microsoft.com/en-us/azure/aks/?msclkid=4da39951a26011ec979b26c5ce45d5b1.

File Structure Validation
Folders and Files Added

Before moving forward, we should review that the files are in the correct locations. If not, you should move them now. Otherwise, the CI/CD deployment may not work correctly. The pipeline files (Continuous-delivery.yaml, Continuous-Integration.yaml) and the deployment.yaml file are required. The _create-azure-resources directory is for housekeeping. _manifests is where we store the scripts that support the pipeline deployment.

Figure 9-4. *GitHub repo file structure. A top-level view of the repo structure*

In Figure 9-4, we can see the directories and top-level files added. In this view, we can see the files and folder structure added. From top to bottom:

- .github/workflows
- _create-azure-resources
- _manifests
- Dockerfile

Figure 9-5. *.github/workflows. Displays the files in the workflows directory*

The .github/workflows file structure should resemble Figure 9-5. This directory contains the CI/CD pipeline scripts. The files are

- Continuous-delivery.yaml

- Continuous-integration.yaml

Figure 9-6. *_manifests. Displays the files in the _manifests directory*

The _manifests file structure should resemble Figure 9-6. This directory contains the file(s) supporting the deployment pipeline. The file is

- deployment.yaml

Secrets for Deployment

We need to log into the Azure Portal to create and gather information to populate our JSON secret file. The JSON file we will make is as follows:

```
{
  "clientId": "xxxxxxxxxxxxxxxxxxxxxxxxxxxxxxxxxxx",
  "clientSecret": " xxxxxxxxxxxxxxxxxxxxxxxxxxxxxxxxxxx ",
  "subscriptionId": " xxxxxxxxxxxxxxxxxxxxxxxxxxxxxxxxxxx ",
  "tenantId": " xxxxxxxxxxxxxxxxxxxxxxxxxxxxxxxxxxx "
}
```

Service Principle Name (SPN)

SPNs are identities that are given a specific role. For example, we will create one to associate with our application. It will provide the application access to deploy and modify the resources. Using a SPN provides additional security since it narrows the access permitted by the application.

To make the SPN, we start by going to the Azure Portal, `https://portal.azure.com`. Once you sign in, we need to walk through a series of steps to gather information and save it to our secrets.

1. Open Azure Active Directory (AAD).

   a. Click App registrations and then select New registration.

   b. Name it appropriately so that it can be found later. For example, the one named for this book is "orleansbasics-app" and click Register.

   c. *Copy the Application (client) ID to the JSON file.*

   d. Next, click Certificates & secrets from the blade menu (menu on the left).

   e. Select Client secrets and then click New client secret. This is where we will name the secret and provide its life span.

      i. I named the secret "orleansbasics secret" and allowed it to default with a 6-month expiration setting.

   f. The name of the secret will be shown along with the secret id.

      i. Copy the value to the clientSecret in the JSON file.

   You will not be able to retrieve the secret value again once you leave this page.

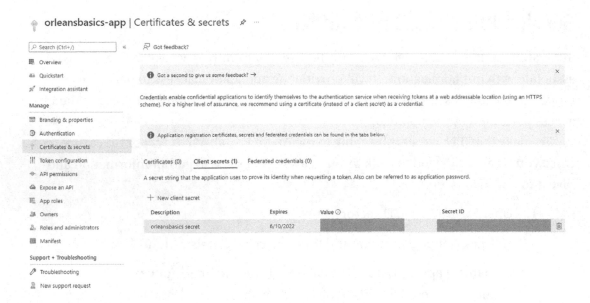

Figure 9-7. *Secret value. Displaying the secret value after adding the client secret*

Figure 9-7 displays the location of the secret value and the secret id. We want to copy the value into the clientSecret field in our JSON file. Do not leave this page before doing so, or the value will be masked, and you will need to create a new secret.

Subscription ID

A subscription is required to associate the application. We can find the subscription by typing "subscription" into the search bar. You will see it highlighted under Services. Select Subscriptions to open the page. Choose the subscription if you have more than one and *copy the "Subscription ID" to the JSON file.*

Tenant ID

A tenant is also required to associate the application. We can find the tenant by typing "tenant" into the search bar. You will see it highlighted under Services. Select Tenant properties to open the page. *Copy Tenant ID into the JSON file.*

Adding Secrets to GitHub

The secrets need to be added to GitHub for the pipeline deployments. We start by going to GitHub and selecting our Orleans repo. If you haven't uploaded the code to GitHub yet, do it now. Once the repo has been established with the code included, we want to select Settings.

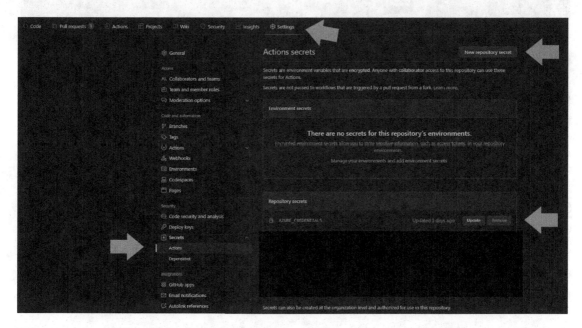

Figure 9-8. *Adding secrets for deployment. The image displays selecting Settings, Actions, New repository secret, and the final result*

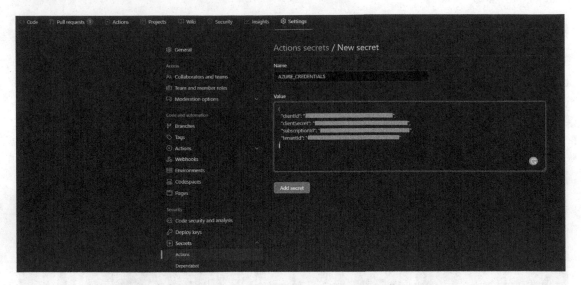

Figure 9-9. *Creating a secret. Secret information is added, and the secret is named*

As shown in Figure 9-8, we will create a secret. First, in the left menu, expand Secrets and click Actions. Then click New repository secret and name it "AZURE_ CREDENTIALS". Next, copy and paste the JSON text into the Value section and click Add secret as shown in Figure 9-9. Once the secret has been added, you will see it deployed at the bottom, as shown in Figure 9-8. This will complete the setup for our automated release.

Automated Deployment

Trigger the Process

Automated deployment is triggered by updates to the main branch. This can be triggered through a pull request or directly updating the main code. An easy way to test this is to add a readme file or modify it in main and commit it. That will show that the build is being triggered, as it should be, and then deployed to Azure.

Figure 9-10. *Actions displaying build status. Shows a completed build from a check-in*

In this section, you should update or add a readme file. Then, commit the change to start the automated build. Figure 9-10 shows us the Actions page in GitHub for our repo. This is where you will see the build and deployment statuses. The image shows that a build was completed. You will see this according to the readme file. It will be an open circle instead of a checkmark while the action is in progress.

Figure 9-11. *Actions showing deployment status. Shows the completed deployment*

Once the build was completed successfully, the deployment action was triggered. In Figure 9-11, we can see that a couple of deployments were previously completed. You will see a similar list, but according to your files. As stated previously, it will be an open ring while processing. It will take a few minutes to complete.

View AKS Status on Azure Portal

Sign in to the Azure Portal and locate the orleansbasics cluster. Here we will find the activity of our cluster.

Figure 9-12. *Azure Portal AKS monitoring. This section displays the activity of the node pools in our cluster*

After finding the Orleans cluster, select the monitor in the middle of the page. It will look like Figure 9-12. Here we can see the activity of our newly deployed application.

AKS Load Balancer

The load balancer is where we locate the external connectivity. We use this address to communicate with our application from outside the cluster.

Figure 9-13. *Load balancer. This image displays the external IP address*

Locate the Kubernetes load balancer and click the resource to open its page. Next, select Frontend IP configuration as shown in Figure 9-13. The external IP address is the highlighted item that states Kubernetes. In my example, the IP address is 20.75.251.187.

Dashboard

If you choose to add the dashboard to Orleans as depicted in Chapter 8, we can display it here. The default port for the dashboard is 8080. Therefore, the address used for my example is 20.75.251.187:8080.

Deploy

Now you can add the connection strings to the database and storage accounts for grain persistence and reminders.

That's it. We have resources provisioned and successful deployment. Outstanding job! It is a decent amount of work to set up automated pipelines; however, it reduces overhead in the future. Nothing will be missed as you extend the pipeline with environments, testing, and additional tools. Also, it's effortless to commit, which autotests and deploys. Finally, it minimizes the time on users and overhead on developers while setting standards that must be passed before being made public.

Here, you can set up another service in the cluster or external to the cluster. For example, you can create a rest service that deals directly with Orleans. That will remove the need for the applications to include and maintain the Orleans libraries and specific interfaces. Instead, that can call a restful service that interfaces with Orleans. It is an extra hop on the network, so it is determined by the need of the application(s).

I genuinely hope you enjoyed setting this up as much as I did writing it. I have a passion for DevSecOps and love sharing my passion with others. Also, this setup can be reused for other projects.

Additional Orleans Troubleshooting Information

Like any application, we can and will run into issues. The Orleans team had the forethought to include failing deployment scenarios. In the event of a problem that displays Orleans-specific errors during deployment, you might find the solution here: `https://dotnet.github.io/orleans/docs/deployment/troubleshooting_deployments.html`.

Summary

In this chapter, we discussed a lot.

We started with compatible grains. Compatible grains need to match the method signature and accessibility. Also, we discussed databases that Orleans supports with grain persistence, including Azure Storage, Amazon DynamoDB, and Microsoft SQL Server. However, the Orleans Contribution GitHub supports many more. Additionally, the membership table is supported by many tools such as Azure Table Storage, SQL Server, and Apache ZooKeeper.

Then we walked through the initial hosting setup. Here we reviewed four files that were initially posted here: `https://github.com/ReubenBond/hanbaobao-web`. The files are used to set up the Azure resources and then deploy our application to them. We took the files and broke them into maintainable sections while partially rewriting them and creating the pipeline files as listed in the following:

- .github/workflows

  - This folder is recognized by GitHub and will be checked for deployment scripts.

  - Here we will add

    - Continous-delivery.yaml

      - This is the script that deploys our work to AKS.

    - Continous-integration.yaml

      - This is the script that builds our code and runs the unit tests.

- _create-azure-resources

  - This folder houses the scripts that create the resources in Azure. We have them written in Bash and PowerShell.

    - Bash_resource_provision.sh

    - Pwsh_resource_provision.ps1

- _manifests

  - This folder contains detailed information about our deployment.

    - Deployment.yaml

- \<root directory\>

  - This is the base folder that contains all the files in the repo.

    - Dockerfile

      - Commands to build a docker image

First, we set up our folder and file structure. Then, we ran the provision file to set up logical locations to store the resources and set up the cluster to run our application. This provided us the resources to deploy our application.

Afterward, we set up a pipeline in GitHub to run every time there is a commit. This makes it easy to keep the latest software builds tested and hosted. Next, the commit should take it to the Dev environment in the real world. Finally, several physical or logical environment stages should be used for testing before the production release. These can be added in the future as the pipeline is extended.

Then, we checked the AKS cluster and viewed the monitoring section to see how the node pools performed. Next, we gathered the external IP address from the load balancer and concluded that if you added the dashboard, you could view it from the \<public IP address\>:8080. Also, since the resources are available, you can now connect the reminder and the grain persistence to the storage account.

Now, we have written and deployed our first Orleans application. Additional services can connect to our service from outside the cluster, or you can release extra applications within the cluster. It depends on the requirement and services and if it makes sense housing them in the same cluster. This is an excellent starting point as anything you add and commit can be immediately available for public consumption. Also, you can take these learnings and deploy them with ease.

Bravo.

## CHAPTER 10

Conclusion

Throughout this book, we discussed how Orleans originated to meet the needs of cloud development and to take advantage of the decentralized structure. In addition, Orleans was created to make decentralized development easier for developers to learn by removing a majority of the low-level work through the Orleans framework, such as virtual actors.

Afterward, we dove into the lifecycles and how they reduce overhead for developers. For example, the framework monitors the grains and keeps them active in memory or decommissions them and persists them in a database. We also compared Orleans with Akka, which is a great framework, but we could see the overhead that Orleans removes compared with Akka.

Once we discussed what makes Orleans unique and an excellent frameworkc, we jumped into design comparisons. This was done to help developers without an actor model background to view it side-by-side with monolithic and microservice patterns. We also discussed how Orleans could enhance the legacy and microservice designs.

From here, we dived into the project setup and development. We covered a lot of commonly used items, such as how grains are set up and the dashboard I wanted to focus based on Orleans that you will reuse in many future projects. From there, you can dive into more intermediate and advanced items as your projects require them. The vital aspect is to take away core items of structure and base application set up to be tested and monitored. You will have a solid basis to take into future projects and implementation to begin the Orleans journey.

Origins

Orleans was created to be able to handle interactive parallel transactions by the trillions while being immensely scalable. Unfortunately, traditional three-tier microservices did not make this requirement an easy task. Actor models inherently supported most of the needs; however, there wasn't a framework available that supported easy development for most programmers.

T. Nelson, *Introducing Microsoft Orleans*, https://doi.org/10.1007/978-1-4842-8014-0_10

After being developed, it was initially used with video games – such as *Halo 3, 4* and *Gears of War* – which showcased the durability and ability of the framework. There are many more applications that can be showcased, but decided on these titles since they are AAA titles and are very well known. It was able to scale to 120 servers that were being 90% utilized without errors (Bernstein & Bykov, 2016). Recall that the 120 servers was not the limit of Orleans, but it was the maximum required by Halo. As we talk about how Orleans interconnects with and grows in networking magnitude such as silos connecting and becoming cluster which then clusters can talk to other cluster which form multi-clusters.

Introduction of Microsoft Orleans

Orleans adheres to actor model principles that have been built into the framework which reduce the burden for developers. Low-level complexities, such as lifecycles, have been supported by the framework. As a result, it allows applications to be created quicker and lowers the risk of errors. Also, Orleans was built to enable a single developer to create and modify the entire application individually, compared with technologies such as Akka, where a team of distribution experts would be required to design and execute the application, which consumes time and development budgets.

Many tools are packed into the framework, such as persistence handling, failure handling, streaming, resource management, health monitoring, and caching. Based on the model and running in memory, various patterns can reduce the requirement for third-party tools such as caching, where a grain can contain the latest query results. Since it is already stored in memory, a call to the grain can prevent a database call.

As a bonus, Orleans has been heavily vetted by the industry since it has been used in 2010. It has supported heavily used projects such as *Halo*, starting in 2011. It has been proven dependable and is constantly being updated through open source, headed by a Microsoft team.

Lifecycles

The lifecycles are one of the primary differences between other actor model frameworks and virtual actors. Orleans takes the unique task of maintaining the lifecycles of the grains. As a result, it removes the risk of accidental coding mishaps and lets us get set up faster. When using Orleans, we spend very little time – in comparison with other actor model frameworks – in the initial building stage of the application. Since Orleans was established in 2010 and used in many prominent and highly visible applications, it has proven trustworthy for enterprise development. The grain lifecycle states move between

1. Activating the grain

2. Being active in memory

3. Deactivating the grain

4. Being persisted in the database

Orleans determines when to deactivate and persist the grain of its own accord, or it can be configured as we see fit. Having this built into the framework allows us to set up the interface and grain logic with minimal code. For example, we do not need to place end-of-life timers or checks for each grain to prevent and persist them when they are no longer in use. Ultimately, we do not need to build the orchestration.

The silo has its lifecycle, which is not as prominent for development; however, it is based on the startup, hosting, and shutdown of the silo. Therefore, the silo running stages are not as relevant to us as coded through the NuGet package. It does help to know the steps for troubleshooting; however, our concern lies with the configuration of data sources, grains, reminders, etc.

Comparisons

The comparison sections were meant to help developers who are coming from the monolithic and microservice patterns understand how Orleans can tie into these patterns. Orleans is not a silver bullet; however, it can be advantageous in many scenarios. Using Orleans can enhance the capabilities of the back end. To understand how Orleans can support these designs, we dove into the history of how they came into being, side-by-side views, and how Orleans can enhance the architecture.

As the Internet has grown, so has global clientele, application development adapted to support the needs. To help explain the evolution due to demand, we used the examples of monolithic services, microservices, and Orleans. However, monolithic applications require the support and synchronizations of multiple teams, which can hinder the deployment ready speed.

Monolithic applications may be thought of as dinosaurs, and many of them are. However, they do have their place. Monolithic services can run faster by not having to pass messages within the network to complete the process. Also, it can be less costly than microservices depending on its growth and how it is maintained. For instance, a monolithic application will require a single pipeline vs. several for each microservice. On the other hand, monolithic services are not as flexible or as scalable at the same rate of microservices and might need significant work to add features. Monoliths may also take additional backend cross-team support in planning, execution sequences, and deployment before release, which can burden time to market and maintainability. Also, running over on deadlines can easily lead to tech debt with "just get it done" coding techniques. Tech debt isn't specific to monolithic development but be prevalent throughout any codebase.

Microservices were created by decoupling the monolithic applications into more minor scoped services. Microservices allowed technologies such as horizontal scaling to increase and decrease instances as user demand dictates. Also, services can be deployed globally and are decentralized. In addition, third-party tools such as caching are sometimes required to reduce the stress on database queries and reduce latency. As mentioned previously, there is a price to pay – the speed of sending payloads through the network, maintaining the scope of each service, individual pipeline, and deployment needs. Finally, each application has a finite number of transactions that it can sustain simultaneously and scale based on its host. In contrast, Orleans scales the grains hosted inside the runtime and communicates in the cluster through TCP, and each silo is a single pipeline.

Orleans uses the silo as we use cloud hosting for many things such as scaling in/out based on traffic and using managed services such as caching. It reduces the number of security points that a message must pass through between microservices with API Management since it lives within the same cluster/silo. API Management is an authentication tool that determines if the message can be passed to another service and is commonly found in cloud design. It can be used to authenticate every message given to each service, including microservices. Additionally, Orleans can scale significantly to the point of trillions of messages.

Project Structure

We created our own project from scratch to understand how Orleans starts, expands, is maintained, and can be deployed. We coded the silo, a client, grains, and interfaces to set up the initial project. These are used as a basis for any project, and as you feel comfortable, it will become second nature. Each of these items is a separate project and is created as a project type:

1. *Interfaces* – Library

2. *Grains* – Library

3. *Silo* – Console application

4. *Client* – Console application

We started with the Interfaces project since it defines the key type, method requirements from the grain that it will be associated with, and how the client can call the grain. The Interfaces project is a library project and will expand with time as new requirements are added to the application.

Next, we created the grains. The grains are where we implement our business logic and will be the primary future focal work section. Luckily, grains can be extended or short-living, and some can grow fairly large. When I initially started working with Orleans, I took it as the mindset that it is an orchestration framework for nano-services (grains); however, I realized this wasn't the case. It can support that design if it meets the requirements, but Orleans is not bound to size requirements.

We added the NuGet packages to our projects. This lets Orleans run, orchestrate, and communicate. Then we added the grain interface that defines the grain requirements and the grain ID type. We created a grain to accept a string message and append a DateTime to the response. The client was created and called the grain with the interface and grain ID to make the request. The silo performs the magic of initializing to passing the message to the appropriate grain.

A few points to recall about silos are that they

- Orchestrate the grains by determining their lifecycle state

- Determine the location of persistence

- Allow connectivity to silos within the cluster and external applications, such as our client

- Connect to other silos to create a cluster

- Monitor health of other silos in a cluster

The silo is where we register the IoC and define where items should be persisted. Silos are also able to communicate with one another, which forms a multi-cluster. Our initial setup is a single silo that uses memory as its persisted state. This is common when development since we have not set up the database yet or do not need one for testing. Of course, we can always set up a database locally or call out one, depending on your company's policies.

Finally, our client was created where we made a call to a grain. When making the call, we defined the grain string ID. Next, we passed a message to the grain, appended a string, and then passed a response.

This setup walked us through the base Orleans application, and we were able to validate it successfully. This was an excellent start for us to get acquainted with the project layout, NuGet packages, and an introductory call that walks through the system.

Timers and Reminders

Timers and reminders are used to create scheduled calls. Orleans has implemented this within the framework, so we do not have to rely on the platform or another application/ API specifically designed to make reoccurring scheduled requests. There is a difference between timers and reminders where timers are

- Meant to be run more often (seconds to hours)

- Not durable if there is a failure

- Needed to be restarted upon failure

Timers are excellent for events that are frequent in nature. For instance, you load a website containing stocks that you would like the data refreshed every 30 seconds. A timer can be created to call on the method to gather the updated results ultimately displayed to the user.

What if it is mission-critical and re-occurring, such as an email notification to present current system health to teams? Reminders are durable and will be saved to the database to run after a failure. The cluster will check for a reminder in the database if reminders were added and trigger events. This removes the need for a manual call to start reminders whenever there is a failure or a silo has been stopped.

Reminders are used for

- Longer times between frequency (minutes to days)

- Durability to live beyond the lifetime of the cluster

- Automatically starting once a cluster is started

Reminders and timers can be used in conjunction to extend them beyond the life of the cluster. The persisted reminders can start after the silo is restarted and then can trigger the timers. This removes the need to retrigger individual timers to start them again upon the silo creation. This allows the silo to restart all of the timers after a failure without relying on an additional tool to initialize the timer calls.

Unit Tests

Unit tests should be baked into development as they allow us to prove working methods as we build our systems. If you were in engineering, then you can think of them as doing proofs as you work. You validate the work during development and likely reduces stress in the long term from unintended results, especially during the release. It is a common practice and well suited for DevSecOps as it is commonly used to help validate before deployment to servers. In DevSecOps, there is usually a unit test percentage coverage set for release. The higher the coverage percentage, the easier it is to obtain approval for release, otherwise more manual testing might be required.

Several common unit testing frameworks are in use, such as Microsoft Test, NUnit, and xUnit. You may have heard of NUnit, a unit testing framework. xUnit, built by the same creators of NUnit, has replaced NUnit with a better framework for testing is and was built to reduce things like code redundancy (Sheth, 2021). For Orleans, we use xUnit rather than the Microsoft testing framework due to support, and seen used by the Orleans creators here: `https://dotnet.github.io/orleans/docs/implementation/testing.html`, that allows us to create the cluster fixture, along with the testing silo. We can create a testing silo that can be customized to our needs. Each of these frameworks is time-tested and has been used throughout a massive amount of projects.

To set up the unit tests, we created specific grains to be tested along with the testing silo. Then we made unit tests and ran them through the Visual Studio test runner. This is emphasized since it is the same tactic we use when writing tests for any application.

Granted, it might be another testing framework minus the test silo, but the process is the same. When I initially learned how to set up unit testing in Orleans, I was thrilled about the familiarity of the process.

There are two primary ways to test Orleans:

- Hosted testing

- Isolated testing

We worked with hosted testing as we set up the testing host. This supplants the real silo for our testing needs and allows us to customize it as needed, such as setting up reminders that are not stored in the database. This is my preferred way of testing; however, it is up to you to discover your favorite.

Isolated testing takes advantage of mocks and fakes. This removes the need to use a testing silo since we would create fabrications of the grains/results to derive the response from the method we are testing. For instance, if you want to test a method based on a database query result, we would mock the database and predefine the result to gather. The unit test will assert if the expected result from the method response matches. Mocking is terrific to remove external calls, tools, and external upkeep. The mock response will always return the response that is given to it within the code.

Orleans Dashboard

The Orleans Dashboard is a visual representation of the state of the application. It is effortless to implement by adding the OrleansDashboard Nuget package and registering the dashboard and automatic grain discovery with the IoC. Once the application is started, we can view the dashboard at http://{address}:8080. *It is built for developer support as they are working on projects and is not intended to replace production monitoring tools (Microsoft, n.d.).*

The dashboard displays

- Summary, silo, grain pages:

  - Total grain activations

    - A holistic view of the grains

  - Total active silos

    - A holistic view of the silos

- Error rate

- Request amount

- Response time

- Summary page

  - Method summary overviews that link to the individual methods to support further analysis

    - Most called methods

    - Methods with most exceptions

    - Methods with the highest latency

- Grains

  - Total activations

  - Individual grain graphs that display

    - Error rate

    - Request amount

    - Response time

- Silos

  - A snapshot row that displays

    - Silo address

    - Silo health

    - Silo uptime

    - Grain activation per silo

  - Mapping of silos by update zones and fault zones

  - Grain, CPU, memory usage

  - Profiling graph

    - Number of requests

    - Failed requests

    - Average latency

- Reminders

  - Number of total reminders

  - List of reminders that can be filtered by metadata such as the reminder name, method name, or time period

- Log stream

  - Displays the current semi-real-time logging

The dashboard allows users to view the current state of the applications quickly. One item that I like the most about the dashboard, other than it being valuable out of the box and having the ability to be customized, is it can be shared with external monitoring teams. It allows an enterprise to be transparent across groups with performance and stability. The development team can share the dashboard and stream the logs to enterprise logging tools, such as Splunk.

Deployment

Deployment – in my opinion – is crucial for development and should be included in all development books. Otherwise, how do developers move their applications from local machines to hosted servers? Not everyone is aware of how to deploy, and perhaps the extent is publishing from Visual Studio which negates gate checks. So often, the work is done and handed to DevOps teams or individuals to discover solutions based on specs. DevSecOps shouldn't be seen as an outside siloed team and should be incorporated into the development team(s). If you are a single developer and trying to build your own tools for personal or business use cases, it is hard to display its solution for real-life scenarios. I wanted to include the complete cycle of software development, which should include deployment. It will allow you to understand how pipelines are created and set up your own automated deployment.

To follow through with this ideology, we learned how to create a pipeline that deploys our silo to Azure Kubernetes. The pipeline allows us to:

1. Deploy when we are happy with our local development

2. Deploy to the server

3. Deploy from a GIT repository

4. Validate the build before deployment

We develop locally and save our work to the GIT repo. Depending on the automation settings you choose, it may deploy as GIT commits are made or when you decide to trigger a deployment. Also, it removes the bottleneck of the limited users with server access if you are manually deploying.

Our pipeline is triggered on a GIT commit, which allows the new code to be saved in the repo. Next, the CI section of the pipeline will build the code and save the artifact. Finally, the CD pipeline will move the artifact to the server and configure settings as needed.

Every time we make a change to our application and commit it, then it will be deployed in this manner. This can be handy for rapid development and prototyping. Security items can be added to the pipeline for scanning and unit test percentages before deployment. These added items can save you from a lot of heartache in the future. A strong DevSecOps infrastructure at the start of a project or in the initial stages of starting a business will remove a significant amount of reworking workflows during the development time and possibly reduce the refactoring of code. The earlier that it is implemented, the less likely it is to rework items for company-wide deployment acceptance.

Future Aspects

Orleans is still growing. It has been implemented in multiple organizations, and it can be implemented in many more. The future of Orleans is bright with its proven track record and ease of implementation. However, most of the use cases are dependent on the creative nature of the solution, have it match the recommendations of to use of Orleans, and know about Orleans.

For instance, teams, such as DevOps and monitoring, can create custom implementation on a holistic scale that support organization implementation standards. Third-party applications and agents can be implemented differently. IoT, messaging, and game development can be developed with the Orleans back end for various sections.

The future of Orleans rests in the hands of the community, open source contributions, and seeing implementations in this constantly changing field. During the writing of this book, Orleans version 4 is being developed. There are so minor changes grain naming, but the foundation remains the same. Perhaps by the time this book is published it will be released as GA.

There is much more to learn, and new features are being added. Take this knowledge and build your own application and attempt to update it. We hope this book helps you to think about development in a new light. This book was meant to add another tool to your belt to be called into action when the use case arises and I trust that it succeeded.

References

3-Tier Architecture. (2019, November 17). Retrieved from Slidershare: `https://www.slideshare.net/datacenters/3tier-architecture`

Actor Model. (2019, December 11). Retrieved from Wikapedia: `https://en.wikipedia.org/wiki/Actor_model`

Agha, G. (1986). *Actors: A Model of Concurrent Computation in Distributed Systems (MIT Press) New edition.* Cambridge, Massachusetts: The MIT Press.

Astbury, R., Gristwood, D., Bobrov, B., Buttigieg, A., Konecki, J., & ksuszka. (n.d.). *Orleans Design Patterns.* Retrieved from Orleans Community Contributions: `https://github.com/OrleansContrib/DesignPatterns`

Astbury, R., Stehle, S., Melnikov, I., Dodson, K., Hammett, R., & Krick, F. (2021, December 30). *Orleans Dashboard.* Retrieved from Orleans Community Contributions: `https://github.com/OrleansContrib/OrleansDashboard`

Athinanthny. (2019, December 19). *Overview of Service Fabric on Azure.* Retrieved from Microsoft: `https://docs.microsoft.com/en-us/azure/service-fabric/service-fabric-overview`

Bernstein, P., & Bykov, S. (2016, October 25). Retrieved from: `https://ieeexplore.ieee.org/document/7676196`

Bernstein, P., Bykov, S., Geller, A., Kliot, G., & Thelin, J. (2014, March 24). *Orleans: Distributed Virtual Actors for Programmability and Scalability.* Retrieved from Microsoft: `https://www.microsoft.com/en-us/research/publication/orleans-distributed-virtual-actors-for-programmability-and-scalability`

Burckhardt, S. (2014). *Principles of Eventual Consistency, Foundations and Trends® in Programming Languages: Vol. 1.* Norwell, MA: now publishers inc. Retrieved from Microsoft Research: `https://www.microsoft.com/en-us/research/publication/principles-of-eventual-consistency/`

Candeias, J. (2019, July 14). *How To Unit Test Framework Services In Orleans.* Retrieved from On Distributed Computing: `https://jorgecandeias.github.io/2019/07/14/how-to-unit-test-framework-services-in-orleans/`

© Thomas Nelson 2022
T. Nelson, *Introducing Microsoft Orleans*, https://doi.org/10.1007/978-1-4842-8014-0

REFERENCES

Cassar, I., & Francalanza, A. (2016, June 01). *On Implementing a Monitor-Oriented Programming Framework for Actor Systems*. Retrieved from SpringerLink: `https://link.springer.com/chapter/10.1007/978-3-319-33693-0_12`

Erlang Programming Language. (2019, December 11). Retrieved from Erlang: `https://www.erlang.org/`

Hamon, A. (2019, April 04). *Do the Math: Scaling Microservices Applications with Orchestrators*. Retrieved from Toptal: `https://www.toptal.com/devops/scaling-microservices-applications`

Kambalyal, C. (2004, November 9). *3-Tier Architecture*. Retrieved from Sushil Consultants Inc.: `https://channukambalyal.tripod.com/NTierArchitecture.pdf`

Lee, E. A. (2003, September 24). *Model-driven development - from object-oriented design to actor-oriented design*. Retrieved from CirteSeer: `http://citeseerx.ist.psu.edu/viewdoc/summary?doi=10.1.1.230.1295`

Mankevich, R. (2013, August 27). *Actor Model description*. Retrieved from Rami On The Web: `https://ramionweb.blogspot.com/2013_08_01_archive.html`

Mauersberger, L. (2019, January 29). *Microservices: What They Are and Why Use Them*. Retrieved from Leanix: `https://www.leanix.net/en/blog/a-brief-history-of-microservices`

Microsoft. (2018, 04 02). *Orleans – Virtual Actors*. Retrieved from Microsoft Research: `https://www.microsoft.com/en-us/research/project/orleans-virtual-actors/publications/`

Microsoft. (n.d.). *Cluster Management in Orleans*. Retrieved from Microsoft Orleans Website: `https://dotnet.github.io/orleans/docs/implementation/cluster_management.html`

Microsoft. (n.d.). *Compatible grains*. Retrieved from Microsoft Orleans Website: `https://dotnet.github.io/orleans/docs/grains/grain_versioning/compatible_grains.html#:~:text=Compatible%20grains%20When%20an%20existing%20grain%20activation%20is,the%20actual%20version%20of%20the%20grain%20are%20compatible.`

Microsoft. (n.d.). *Grain Directory*. Retrieved from Microsoft Orleans Website: `https://dotnet.github.io/orleans/docs/host/grain_directory.html`

Microsoft. (n.d.). *Grain Persistence*. Retrieved from Microsoft Orleans Website: `https://dotnet.github.io/orleans/docs/grains/grain_persistence/index.html`

Microsoft. (n.d.). *Handling Failures*. Retrieved from Microsoft Orleans Website: `https://dotnet.github.io/orleans/docs/deployment/handling_failures.html`

Microsoft. (n.d.). *Heterogeneous silos.* Retrieved from Microsoft Orleans Website: https://dotnet.github.io/orleans/docs/host/heterogeneous_silos.html

Microsoft. (n.d.). *Immediate Confirmation.* Retrieved from Microsoft Orleans Website: https://dotnet.github.io/orleans/docs/grains/event_sourcing/immediate_vs_delayed_confirmation.html?q=concurrency%20guarantee

Microsoft. (n.d.). *JournaledGrain Diagnostics.* Retrieved from Microsoft Orleans Website: https://dotnet.github.io/orleans/docs/grains/event_sourcing/journaledgrain_diagnostics.html

Microsoft. (n.d.). *Messaging Delivery Guarantees.* Retrieved from Microsoft Orleans Website: https://dotnet.github.io/orleans/docs/implementation/messaging_delivery_guarantees.html

Microsoft. (n.d.). *Orleans is a cross-platform framework for building robust, scalable distributed applications.* Retrieved from Microsoft Orleans Website: https://dotnet.github.io/orleans/docs/index.html

Microsoft. (n.d.). *Persistence.* Retrieved from Microsoft Orleans Website: https://dotnet.github.io/orleans/docs/grains/grain_persistence/index.html

Microsoft. (n.d.). *Server Configuration.* Retrieved from Microsoft Orleans Website: https://dotnet.github.io/orleans/docs/host/configuration_guide/server_configuration.html

Microsoft. (n.d.). *Silo Lifecycle.* Retrieved from Microsoft Orleans Website: https://dotnet.github.io/orleans/docs/host/silo_lifecycle.html

Microsoft. (n.d.). *Tutorial One - Creating a Minimal Orleans Application.* Retrieved from Microsoft Orleans Website: https://dotnet.github.io/orleans/docs/tutorials_and_samples/tutorial_1.html

Microsoft. (n.d.). *Who Is Using Orleans?* Retrieved from Microsoft Orleans Website: https://orleanscn.github.io/orleans/Community/Who-Is-Using-Orleans.html

Microsoft. (n.d.). *Why Orleans Streams?* Retrieved from Microsoft Orleans Website: https://dotnet.github.io/orleans/docs/streaming/streams_why.html

Oloruntoba, S. (2020, September 21). *SOLID: The First 5 Principles of Object Oriented Design.* Retrieved from Conceptual Article: https://www.digitalocean.com/community/conceptual_articles/s-o-l-i-d-the-first-five-principles-of-object-oriented-design

Orleans is a cross-platform framework for building robust, scalable distributed applications: Microsoft Orleans Documentation. (2019, December 11). Retrieved from Microsoft Orleans Website: https://dotnet.github.io/orleans/

REFERENCES

Patent Issued for Actor Model Programming (USPTO 10,768,902). (2020). *In Information Technology Newsweekly*, 2260.

Sheth, H. (2021, March 22). *NUnit vs. XUnit vs. MSTest: Comparing Unit Testing Frameworks In C#*. Retrieved from Lambdatest: `https://www.lambdatest.com/blog/nunit-vs-xunit-vs-mstest/`

Sukanyamsft, Doyle, E., Pickett, W., DCtheGeek, Nickomang, Hu, J., . . . seanmck. (2019, December 19). *Introduction to Service Fabric Reliable Actors*. Retrieved from Microsoft Docs: `https://docs.microsoft.com/en-us/azure/service-fabric/service-fabric-reliable-actors-introduction`

Index

A, B

Actor model, 1
  definition, 5
  Erlang, 10
  features, 10, 12
  frameworks, 4
  grain lifecycle, 9
  lifecycles, 7
  memory, 8
  message flow, 6
  production uses/history, 12
  rules, 14
  single developer, 10
Atomic, consistent, isolated, and durable (ACID) transactions, 8
Azure environment, 139, 145
Azure Kubernetes, 186
Azure table
  access keys, 106, 107
  adding table, 105
  create resource, 100
  deployment completion, 105
  menu items, 100, 101
  search results, resources, 101
  selection, 102
  storage setup, 104
  tables blade, 105, 106

C

Client
  GrainIds, 82

  grain lifecycle, 75–77
  running, 80, 81
Cloud agnosticism, 8
Cloud computing, 2, 4, 17
Clouds, 8, 24
Cluster management, 141, 142
Compatible grains, 139, 140, 174
Composition, 67, 68
Continuous integration and continuous delivery (CI/CD)
  Azure table, 145
  Continuous-delivery.yaml, 161, 163, 164
  Continuous-Integration.yaml, 159–161
  deployment types, 144
  DevOps, 145
  environments, 142, 143
  integration script, 158
  pipeline
    creation, 142, 146
    naming, 158
  scrum, 144
  sites, 143, 144
  SQL Server, 145

D

Database Administrators (DBAs), 141
Database handling, 141
Deployment
  automated
    AKS Status, 171, 172

© Thomas Nelson 2022
T. Nelson, *Introducing Microsoft Orleans*, https://doi.org/10.1007/978-1-4842-8014-0

Deployment (*cont.*)
 connection strings, 173
 dashboard, 173
 load balancer, 172
 Orleans, 173
 rest service, 173
 triggering, 170, 171
Azure CLI, 147, 148
files
 Deployment.yaml, 154–158
 Dockerfile, 152, 153
file structure validation, 165, 166
GitHub, 169, 170
secrets, 166–168
DevOps, 23, 52, 59, 186, 187
DevOps pipelines, 113
DevSecOps, 39, 173, 183, 186, 187

E

Erlang, 5, 7, 10

F

Functional testing, 64, 143

G

GIT commit, 187
GitHub, 27, 169, 170
Globally Unique Identities (GUIDs), 6
Grain, 7–10, 18, 19, 21, 23–27, 29, 31–34,
 40, 41, 44–47, 50, 54, 69
communication
 CallingGrain.cs, 86
 definition, 82
 GrainInterfaces project, 85
 interface, 83

IUnitTestingGrain, 83
 setup, 88
 Silo, 87
 testing, 83
 UnitTestingGrain, 84
interface, 72
Grain Call Filters, 34
Grain lifecycle, 179
 call filters, 34
 definition, 29
 framework, 31, 32
 reentrancy, 32
 services, 33
 stateless workers, 33
 tasks/grains, 33

H

Heterogeneous silos, 45
Honeywell devices, 12

I, J

IGrainWithStringKey, 11

K

Kubernetes, 8, 18, 23, 49, 58, 61, 63, 65,
 157, 172, 186

L

Load tests, 64

M

Microservices, 3, 18, 23, 24, 47, 50–54, 59,
 61–66, 177, 179, 180

Microsoft Orleans
    actor model frameworks, 18, 19
    community/constant
        advancements, 22
    definition, 1
    framework, 13, 14
    high elasticity and availability
        characteristics, 17, 18
    multiple hosting solution, 23
    persistence, 26
    resource management/
        expansion, 23, 24
    single developer, 21
    streaming, 25, 26
Monolithic applications, 3
    availability, 58
    business logic complexity, 59–61
    cloud hosting, 54
    definition, 49
    deployment, 63, 64
    Devops, 52
    elasticity, 55–57
    examples, 52
    framework, 50
    legacy applications, 49
    microservice, 53
    scopes, 53
    services, 65, 66
    services/microservices, 51
    silo, 55
Monolithic architectures, 4
Multi-cluster
    eventual consistency, 44
    gateways, 43
    Gossip network, 46
    heterogeneous silos, 45
    journaled grains, 44
    protocol, 43

N

.NET Core libraries, 2, 69
NuGet packages, 4, 21, 27, 71, 181

O

Orleans
    Dashboard, 184, 186
    definition, 177
    Internet, 179
    Microsoft, 178
    project structure, 181
Orleans Dashboard
    additional options, 135, 136
    address, 128
    aggregated lists, 129
    expanding, 136
    grains, 129, 131
    interface, 128, 129
    items, 125
    log stream, 134
    method tracing information, 130, 131
    NuGet package, 127
    page information, 133
    preferences, 134
    reminders, 133
    Silo Program.cs file, 127, 128
    silos, 131, 132
    target framework, 126
Orleans unit testing, 114, 115, 123

P, Q

Provisioning scripts
    Azure CLI, 149
    Bash script, 150, 151
    components, 151
    PowerShell script, 149, 150

R

RAM and processors, 50
Reminders
    benefits, 92
    creation
        IReminderGrain.cs, 98
        Program.cs, 97
        ReminderGrain.cs, 98, 99
        StartSilo method, 97
    Orleans stores, 109
    running, 107–109
"RespondWIthCurrentTime" method, 72

S

Service Principle Name (SPNs), 167, 168
Silo
    code, 75
    grain directory, 36
    grains, 35
    lifecycle, 34
    membership, 41
    Program.cs file, 73, 74
SOLID principles, 8–10, 15
StringKey grain, 89

T

Test Driven Development (TDD), 113, 142
Timers
    benefits, 92
    creation
        Client Program.cs, 94, 95
        ITimerGrain.cs, 92
        TimerGrain.cs, 92, 93

    lifetimes, 91
    vs. reminders, 91
    running, 95, 96
Timers and reminders, 89, 91, 92, 110, 114, 124, 182
Transaction lifecycle
    cluster, 41
    development setup, 38
    silo configuration, 39
    typical configuration, 39

U

Uniform Resource Identifiers (URIs), 6
UnitTesting grains, 88, 89
Unit tests, 183
    additional testing, 123
    CallingGrain Test, 121, 122
    creation, grain, 116
    Orleans, 114, 115
    outcome, 122, 123
    pipelines, 114
    TDD, 113
    Test Cluster
        baseline pattern, 118
        ClusterCollection.cs, 119
        ClusterFixture.cs, 119
        TestSiloConfigurations.cs, 120
        UnitTest.cs, 117, 118
    test runner, 120, 121
    uses, 114

V, W, X, Y, Z

Visual Studio, 23, 68, 70, 152, 182, 186